North American Birds of Prey

North American

GAGE PUBLISHING LIMITED/TORONTO   ONTARIO   CANADA   1980

Birds of Prey

TEXT BY William Mansell PAINTINGS BY Gary Low

Canadian Cataloguing in Publication Data

Mansell, William C., 1908–
  North American birds of prey

Bibliography: p. 175
ISBN 0-7715-9452-6

1. Birds of Prey — North America.   I. Low, Gary,
1948–

QL696.F3M36   598′.9′097   C80-094218-3

1 2 3 4 AP 83, 82, 81, 80

PRINTED AND BOUND IN CANADA

Contents

To my wife,
Millicent,

equally skilled
in the culinary arts
and
in hawk-watching

Foreword

Thanks are due the many who have trod this way in the past. The multitude, a small army, ranges from amateur birders to the highest rank in the hierarchy of ornithologists, those professionals whose names are trailed by sufficient letters to make a new, albeit, badly jumbled alphabet. I would, however, be remiss were I not to single out a few to whom I am, indeed, greatly indebted. James L. Baillie is one, Lester L. Snyder another, both highly esteemed ornithologists and beloved men who left indelible marks on Toronto's Royal Ontario Museum of Zoology and who guided this writer in his most naive years. I am exceedingly grateful to Gerald McKeating, biologist formerly with the Ministry of Natural Resources, for his assistance in preparing the chapters on the peregrine falcon and on pesticides, matters with which he is deeply involved. My older son, Dan, another biologist and manager of the Midhurst District of the same provincial body, ably criticized the scientific veracity of the manuscript without straining the paterfamilias bond. He was also helpful in many other ways. I must also extend my thanks to Eunice Reidel, of William Morrow and Company, Inc., for her helpful suggestions and to the staff of the Royal Ontario Museum, Division of Birds, for unearthing some pertinent data. Of prime importance was the polishing of the text by Colleen Dimson of the editorial staff of Gage Publishing Limited. Finally, fellow author, J. Lloyd Van Camp, whose knowledge of, and long experience in forestry cannot be denied, carried me back many years by marking, in true professorial fashion, my imperfections with the English language. In the final analysis, however, all faults with the text must come to rest on my shoulders. Obviously, the most critical examination of the concomitant plates will reveal that Gary Low's work transcends reproach, an understandable reflection, as lyrics can enhance a song, but the melody has to be there in the first place.

William C. Mansell

MISSISSAUGA, ONTARIO

Preface

Certain difficulties arise over the course of time in the preparation for a book of this nature, the principal problem concerning the observation of all species in their natural habitat. It is an easy matter when one wishes to locate a kestrel or red-tailed hawk, but birds such as the owls of the northern boreal forest, the gyrfalcon and peregrine present a problem either because of their rarity or arduous habitat. Many birders consider themselves extremely fortunate to include the great gray or the hawk owl on their life list, and few indeed have ever included the eastern peregrine falcon because of its near extinct status. Therefore, some of the birds included in this book have been observed as captive specimens in order to achieve accuracy in my paintings.

I wish to thank the following people for their assistance on this project: Glen Murphy of the Royal Ontario Museum, for setting aside certain raptors for my use before they were prepared for the Museum's collection; Katherine and Larry McKeever, founders of the Owl Rehabilitation Research Foundation in Vineland, Ontario, who have kindly given me access to species of owls not readily observed in the wild; Ulrich Watermann who employs the ancient sport of falconry to keep gulls off the runways at the Toronto International Airport for giving me the pleasure of observing falcons in flight; Bret Newsome who helped in the initial presentation of this book; Bill Mansell who has been a pleasure to work with on this project and who continues to astound me with his vast knowledge of birds derived from his extensive field experience. Finally I wish to thank my wife Edith and daughter Erinn, firstly for their encouragement, and secondly for their patience in enduring my long hours of absence while I was painting in my studio.

Gary Low

NEWMARKET, ONTARIO

Introduction

In its general usage, the term "Birds of Prey" has a restricted meaning. A standard encyclopedic dictionary states that such a bird is "an eagle, hawk, vulture, falcon, etc." The same work states that predatory means "of, relating to, or characterized by plundering," or "living by pillaging," very descriptive of the habits of eagles, hawks, etc. But when we inquire into the word predation, we find it is "the act of animals that kill other animals for food." It is this killing to provide sustenance that makes us pause for thought.

For the word "animal," including as it does all forms of life not inanimate, includes such birds as the much eulogized bluebird, an ethereal, gentle species almost as much a bird of prey as an eagle, as only 30 per cent of its food is vegetable matter. Its relative, the familiar and confiding robin, must also be considered a bird of prey. Its taste for earthworms, which are animals, is well known; nor is it averse to the occasional salamander, although the latter's tail may have confused the robin. Others of the same, almost world-wide genus, and our own woodland thrushes, the wood, hermit, Swainson's, gray-cheek and veery, exhibit a similar failing in eyesight on occasion. The oriole and the red-eyed vireo delight our ears with snatches of arias, interspersing these excursions into the world of opera with rapacious onslaughts on such animal life as caterpillars, cutworms, weevils, curculios and the like. Notwithstanding their esthetic musical qualities, the fact that their diet is only about 15 per cent vegetable matter would mean that the so-called "Birds of Prey" do not have exclusive rights to the title.

Splitting hairs, or, more properly, feathers, with a still finer blade, we can safely call *any* bird a "Bird of Prey," for even the most confirmed seed-eater consumes insects, if not periodically through the year, at least in the early stages of its life. Insect life, a food high in protein, is the pablum of the bird world, the food you see being crammed into the maw of a young, quivering-winged sparrow, whose bill will soon reflect all the properties required for husking and splitting seeds. Critical appraisal at this point may justify calling the adult sparrow a bird that engages in predation, because it kills while its young are predatory, and because they live on slaughtered animals.

If we deem a predator one that kills *vertebrate* animals more or less exclusively, we find a good many birds no longer qualify as "Birds of Prey," as their animal food does not include: fishes; frogs, toads or salamanders; snakes, lizards or turtles; mammals, which are those creatures colloquially called animals; and other birds. The problem now is what to do with: loons and kingfishers, whose specialty is fish; herons, that have a penchant for frogs; the roadrunner, a confirmed eater of snakes and lizards; the omnivorous crows, jays and grackles, with their tendency to near cannibalism, as they will eat the callow young of other bird species; and the shrikes, which would subsist entirely on mice and small birds if summer did not bring a recurrence of insects.

As with most popular misconceptions, the term "Birds of Prey," as used by the majority of people, is therefore quite erroneous. A far better term is "Raptor." A raptor, or raptorial bird, is one that seizes its prey with its talons, a method employed by about 4.5 per cent of the world's 8,900 species, give or take a few dozen. This small minority is made up of approximately 281 hawks, an all-embracing term for the vultures, buzzards, eagles, kites, ospreys, falcons *et al*, and 136 owls. Both figures are, as usual in such cases, suspect, and subject to alterations (not necessarily corrections) by leading authorities. Any other bird that aspires to inclusion in the "Birds of Prey" must first master the technique of capturing its food by the foot, not the bill.

Unfortunately, there are certain species which, from their appearance alone if not from the more critical anatomical features, are not wholly raptorial or even predaceous. The palm-nut vulture of Africa makes scant use of vertebrate life, relying instead almost exclusively on parts of the nuts of certain palm trees. The honey-buzzard of the eastern hemisphere is another casual vertebrate eater, preferring instead the actual nests of wasps and bees and the insects and honey they contain. Vultures the world over are predatory but are not given to predation. They do not normally kill, preferring to wait until their food has expired by other means. Nor are their feet truly raptorial, being unable to grasp and therefore to carry. They do, however, use the feet as do other predators when rendering food, holding down a corpse while pulling it apart. They are possibly farthest removed from a true hawk in appearance but, since they, and the palm-nut vulture and honey-buzzard as well, are structurally akin to the other hawks, etc., we must, perforce, include all in that division of birds.

When systematists were proposing fantastic theories and defining improbable relationships, and when taxonomists were adjusting to the binomial nomenclature of that innovator, Carl von Linné, who was not the originator but the one who put it to practical use by systematizing it, it was generally agreed that hawks and owls were related, one group having departed from the norm by developing the art of hunting by night. There was little objection to this arrangement, although scientists of the day were quite aware that the two groups had few common denominators, one of which was a strongly hooked bill set in a soft cere. But their most common bond was the use of talons in grasping prey. In *Cassell's Natural History*, published in 1884, not quite one hundred years ago, we find that F. Bowlder Sharpe grouped the hawks and owls in one order, *Accipitres*, dividing it into three suborders: the owls; the osprey (segregated because of its reversible outer toe); and the hawks.

In 1917, falacious reasoning persisted, for, although the osprey was now included with all other hawks, the American vultures had been given a suborder of their own, still retaining, however, three suborders: hawks, American vultures, and owls. The nomenclaturists of the day gave this order the Latin name *Raptores*.

The modern view puts hawks and their allies, including American vultures and the osprey, in the order *Falconiformes*, the owls in an order of their own, *Strigiformes*, and places the groups far apart in any lineal arrangement, thus emphasizing that the relationship of one group to the other is a distant one.

Fossil evidence, dating back sixty to seventy million years, points to the American vultures, which may not have originated in America at all, as the earliest of the group of raptors, and they, as has been pointed out, do not have a typically raptorial foot. Indeed, some postulate that they are more closely related to the South American seriemas, relatives of the cranes, than they are to the hawks. Hawks, as we know them, seem to have first appeared from thirty to forty million years ago.

The earliest known owl, called *Protostrix mimica*, lived fifty-five to seventy million years before the present. Whether viewed in its fossil state or in some form of reconstruction, it is obviously an owl, far removed structurally, from *Lithornis*, the earliest "American" vulture, which was fossilized in the country we call England. Obviously, the common ancestor of hawks and owls would have had to have lived far earlier than did *Lithornis*.

The hawks and owls vying with early man for relished game and, it must be admitted, carrion, were little different, if any, from our present-day species. Undoubtedly they had a common ancestor of which we have no trace and so far back in history that nothing remotely hominid could have seen it.

While man was evolving from some prosimian form through *Australopithecus* to the present *Homo sapiens* and the dominant creature on earth, other predators, including hawks and owls, were playing similar if subordinate roles, each commanding some thing or group of things living at that time. Many of these rulers and their subjects have departed long since; but some, principally the serfs, are still with us, in a form virtually unchanged over millions of years. These forms that have changed so little are the most numerous and smallest in the world and are the foundations of the ecosystems of today's life. Like a building, or, more precisely, a pyramid, the lowest form supports larger and, in terms of potential for destruction, more powerful forms; and they, larger forms again, the pyramid being topped by the dominant predator in that particular structure, or, as it is called, food-chain.

The largest, longest and most complicated chains originate in the water, for life began in the sea, and flourishes there more than on land. Microscopic plant plankton, floating near the surface of a lake or pond, absorb dissolved nutrients and capture energy directly from the sun. Protozoans and rotifers eat the plankton and are in turn eaten by tiny crustaceans such as water fleas. Predatory insect larvae, larger crustaceans and younger fishes now enter the picture, to serve in turn as food for predatory beetles, water bugs and larger fishes. Frogs and our game fishes, bass and pickerel among them, have their turn, to end up in the stomach of raccoons, otters, mink, herons, loons, kingfishers, ospreys, fish owls and man. Some of these, even man at times, may be displaced and be the dinner instead of the diner, as a hawk may take a mink, one large owl may capture a smaller one, and a man may fall prey to a lion or shark. Fortunately, especially in the latter case, none of these illustrations is habitual.

When an individual dies by other means (starvation, disease or old age), or has been killed but not wholly eaten, its decaying shell is consumed by protozoans which started the cycle in the first place. In fact, the circle is never broken even when the prey is eaten, as its unwanted parts are discharged in the feces of the eater to again receive the attention of protozoans. A food-chain commencing on land is similar in construction but with fewer components.

Some chains are short and relatively simple. In the marshes of Florida, detritus is eaten by apple snails *(Pomacea)*, the only food item of the Everglade kite, which, having no secondary food to turn to, is in danger of extinction through the draining of the marshes and the consequent loss in the numbers of apple snails.

Most food chains, however, are not only lengthy but interdependant. Four-wing saltbrush grows, along with grass, in the prairies of the central United States. Cattle eat both and relish the former. Grasshoppers also eat the grass and are, in turn, eaten by lark buntings. These prairie-loving birds nest in saltbrush and are thus dependent on the habits and numbers of cattle. Paraphrasing George M. Van Dyne (*Frontiers*, Spring, 1978): More cattle means less four-wing saltbrush, resulting in fewer lark buntings, more grasshoppers, less grass, less cattle, back to more four-wing saltbrush. As American kestrels and prairie falcons also eat grasshoppers, with the latter also eating small birds which probably include lark buntings, the prevalence of saltbrush can effect their lives too.

With each block of the pyramidal food chain dependent on one or more below it and, sometimes on one or more blocks of an adjacent pyramid (a feat of engineering unknown to architects!) it is obvious that the removal of one block will seriously weaken the structure, at least above the point of removal. The filling in of marshes and small ponds is a classic example of the destruction of a pyramid from or near the bottom, as such misdirected engineering will bring about the extinction of the very important microscopic life they once held. The removal of saltbrush, referred to in the preceding paragraph, is another example. Happily, the pyramids of life, unlike those of Egypt and Mexico, do have the power to regenerate, but the process is time-consuming, involving thousands, if not millions of years.

In recent years we have seen the process reduced to a short span in the life of man. The new pesticides and germicides that have contributed much to a more pleasant life have one failing. While they eradicate incalculable numbers of the virus, mosquito or other pest they were primarily designed to destroy, they obviously cannot kill off all of them. Some may be so concealed as to be missed by the toxic agent; others may survive because they are an abnormally strong strain. Thus, strong strains continue to be, or are developed from the union of a strong and a "normal" strain, which itself, may produce a stronger strain by mutation. Laboratories are continually striving to develop even stronger death-dealing agents. Complete eradication seems an impossibility.

Even the removal of the apex will bring about the destruction of the chain. The topmost block of the edifice, such as a wolf, lion, hawk or owl, was, in effect, holding down those immediately under it by keeping its members in check. With this control removed, the now-exposed blocks run rampant, their excessive weight (numbers) smothering their immediate supports or creating such an imbalance the whole structure topples on its side, resulting in either chaos or disintegration of the whole.

Within his own lifetime, however, a man may see a new apex develop, or, in the words of present-day biologists, see an already existing species move into an unoccupied niche. That is exactly what took place with the short-eared owl in Hawaii. Until the barn owl was introduced into that island, the short-eared was the only owl found there. It took full advantage of the absence of strigine competitors by exploiting all manner of food sources which in other parts of the world it left to the other kinds of owls sharing its range.

To refer to the work of L. David Mech might seem out of place in a book of birds, as his studies, on Isle Royale, Michigan, were of two mammals, the moose and the wolf. But because they emphasize so strongly the need for population control, and therefore the role of the predator, they are summarized here.

Before the timber wolf became established on that island, the only factors controlling the size of the moose herd were the abundance of its food – browse – and of course, disease, which is related to food scarcity. From 1915 through 1920, the moose population was quite stable, but in the decade following, it increased tenfold. A dramatic die-off, the result of insufficient browse, took place, followed some years later by an increase which showed every indication that the population would again reach the excessive figure of the 1930s. But at this point, the wolf entered the picture, having reached the island by presumably crossing on ice in winter. The wolf-moose population began to balance on a teeter-totter, the fulcrum of which was browse. In a few years, the wolves reduced the herd to a number that could subsist comfortably on the quantity of browse available.

Wolves are continually removing moose from the herd, selecting, as a matter of expediency, those individuals most easily caught. A moose weakened by disease or starvation succumbs to wolf predation before it has much chance, if any, of transmitting that disease to another. Young moose fall prey too, but again, it is the "weak" one, the one not properly camouflaged or protected, or of such temperament as to defy parental injunction to remain hidden. When moose are in short supply, the wolves turn to varying hare, abandoning such secondary food at the first opportunity because less energy is expended in killing one moose than in killing a quantity of hares of equal volume. At all times, wolves control themselves, regulating their population according to the maximum moose herd. The wolf is the upportmost block of a pyramid resting on two others, the bulk of it on the moose block and a small portion on the hare block.

The predation-free deer herds in the Great Swamp National Wildlife Refuge of New

Jersey and in Rondeau Provincial Park in Ontario, have been weakened by disease, the result of starvation through overcrowded conditions. Predation, even in the form of controlled hunting, would restore the herd-browse equilibrium.

Hawks and owls function in the same way, as they, too, are controlling agents, responsible for containing the population of some animals not infrequently considered pests and which cannot be controlled by annual hunting seasons.

As Frank C. Edminster summed it up in his *American Game Birds*: "Predation is merely the tool that nature uses to bring the prey down to the numbers its environment can care for each year. If this agent were to be entirely removed, some other would take its place and the result would be eventually the same."

This book was conceived by the artist Gary Low, who admits to an increased flow of adrenalin when in the presence of a hawk or owl. Had he been painting forty or fifty years ago, it is unlikely that the birds would have been depicted any differently. The bird's fierce mien, with recently caught victim in vise-like grip of piercing talons, would probably have been presented in the same way. But had the author entered into this partnership at that time, the text would have been in a far different vein, for I was nurtured on the prose of Neltje Blanchan, Thomas Nuttall, Olive Thorne Miller, Mabel Osgood Wright, John Burroughs, W. Thornton Burgess and others of that era.

To them, a bird of prey in the shape of an owl or hawk was the epitome of evil, a Satanic creation that feasted on the flesh of others, killing with the fury of a demon from Hell. And, to add to the horror these "evil" birds created, they chose as victims, those most pleasing to man's eye, ear or stomach. As an aside, the writers sometimes referred to the penchant of a certain kind of hawk for loathesome snakes (to them, there were no other kind); or they noted that one owl in particular doted on foul house rats. Such comments were expressed in the same way they might have admitted that Cousin Oscar, whose term of penal servitude had still eleven years to run, had always had an easy rapport with children.

To me, in my early days of birding and bird study, the demise of a bird of prey, that is, a raptor, could only mean that more birds of the kind we liked to have around us would survive. This did not mean that I was abroad from time to time, eliminating such raptors with rifle or shotgun. My excursions into the realm of hunting with firearms was very brief. It did mean that I was a staunch advocate of all that the writers of the turn of the century had to say about, or more properly, against hawks and owls.

About the time I commenced serious bird study, in the early thirties, a new concept was being entertained. All birds were now classified according to food habits, each stuffed neatly into one of three pigeonholes: good, bad or neutral. A good or beneficial species was one whose food tastes ran to crop-, fruit- or grain-destroying insects; or one that destroyed the mouse that ate the grain that made the bread that Jack ate. A bad, or harmful bird was one that habitually feasted on beneficial species, whether bird, mammal or insect. Some birds were considered neutral, a kind of avian drone, their good deeds fairly balancing their bad. Or, perhaps their principal food item was one we humans had little interest in. Apple snails did not appear on our menus, so the Everglade kite lived in that gray zone.

This new attitude did remove the stigma long attached to certain raptors. But, since even the best of us fall from grace now and then, ornithological opinions varied somewhat. It was still evident, however, that all raptors were regarded with a certain amount of suspicion. It was obvious that, while some hawks and owls were given a clean, or, at best, a slightly soiled certificate and while a few were blatantly black-listed, most were living on probation. This suspended judgment was totally ignored by the birds, who continued to catch and eat the same things they always had, things they had been designed to catch in the course of evolution.

As might be expected, I tagged along behind the majority.

Then came the great change and the introduction of the word ecosystem into the language. Some enterprising scientists reasoned that these birds of prey, these raptorial killers, just might have some ulterior purpose and might not be such nuisances after all. Serious study by a growing number of environmentalists and ecologists convinced other professionals, and got through to the laymen. At the present time, only the uneducated, the misanthropes, and those whose despotism limits their perspective, fail to subscribe to the theory.

In brief, the present theory is that birds of prey in common with all predators, remove diseased, weak and genetically inferior animals, thereby keeping both predator and prey populations healthy. To say that I am a subscriber to this theory is an understatement. It is inconceivable that anything is on this earth without a purpose, although the reasons in some cases are cloaked in obscurity.

As mentioned earlier in this chapter, those writing about birds, particularly about birds of prey, have progressed from advocating their wholesale liquidation, through partial extermination, to the present policy of live and let live. I have adopted the latter, but not because I abhor killing, as I have killed, nor because I am a "bird-lover," a term I greatly detest. But I do enjoy birds and appreciate their beauty, even when, as in the crow, it is an unrelieved black; and I revel in their song, or their efforts to create one, wishing, all the while, that my talent for music were greater so that I could incorporate their melodies into a woodland symphony.

In keeping with that policy, I have maligned none of the birds included in this book; nor have I extolled the virtues of the righteous, if, indeed, any can claim such distinction. Rather, I have tried to present them as objects worthy of further study, whose role in the scheme of nature is not to rid us of vermin, an act which would be tantamount to suicide, but to keep that vermin within some degree of tolerance.

There are some organisms whose extinction would make for a happier world. *Anopheles, Culex* and *Aedes,* are genera of mosquitos we could do without. They include the species that either transmit malaria or yellow fever or are simply irritants. We might also include the house mouse *(Mus musculus)* and the Norway rat *(Rattus norvegicus).* And contrary to the opinions of countless nature writers who have bemoaned its loss, we are obliged to include the passenger pigeon, extinct now for sixty-five years. If that bird still existed in but one-tenth its former numbers of billions, scheduled air flights would be impossible. We must regard that bird as the North American species of manna that provided some of the sustenance for the settlers who opened up this continent. Today's world has no place for its fantastic numbers.

There are, however, no valid reasons for the elimination of any of our raptors; nor is any raptor vital to our existence. Some are bound to disappear in time, as man reduces certain habitats to his own real or imagined advantage. But there is no reason to hasten their departure. Instead, as all species are intricably woven into the web of life, there is every reason for man to exert himself and to preserve at least the *status quo*.

While man has made tremendous strides in developing a planned, natural history community (successful fish stocking, for example), he is also learning to research releases thoroughly so as not to duplicate the gaffes of our forefathers who introduced house sparrows and starlings into North America, rabbits into Australia and Russian boar into the Carolinas. Writers around the world have pointed out the harmful effects caused by the proliferation of introduced house sparrows and starlings and the damage to Australian agriculture caused by the introduction of rabbits to that country. Hog wallows now abound in the Carolinas because of the Russian boars introduced there by wealthy sportsmen to provide hunting, and neighboring states may be on the verge of invasion by the dangerous porkers, an obvious detriment to North American environment. Exotic ungulates released on Texas ranches for the shooting pleasure of hunting parties, may also escape, spread and destroy the delicate ecosystems of southern areas. The escape and spread of house finches and monk parrots in the eastern United States is also of great concern to environmentalists in both the United States and Canada, as the possibility of their emulating the expropriating nature of house sparrows and starlings is not entirely remote.

The same, blithe disregard for the far-reaching effects of man's engineering plans is seen in the many water-storing and water-moving projects throughout the world. The Aswan Dam was built amidst dire forebodings, many of which have been fulfilled. Much the same sense of doom precedes the draining of the Sudd in Africa. The negative impact of the James Bay project in Canada's Province of Quebec may be far in excess of its positive factors. And the residents of Colorado and Wyoming are so intent on grabbing every drop of the Platte River by damming it that the people of Nebraska are beginning to realize that very little water may ever reach their state.

Parks Canada, with a mandate to hold public lands in trust for the benefit of present and future Canadians, recently approved the expansion of ski facilities in Riding Mountain National Park, Manitoba. Opposition by leading protagonists of wildlife and environment preservation, who argued that the move contravened national park objectives, led to the preparation of an Environmental Impact Statement by the ski facilities operator. Parks Canada, a public body, would not release this statement to the public it represents.

It is the same Parks Canada that continually sidesteps ordering the cessation of duck shooting at Point Pelee National Park, asserting that the establishment of the park in 1918 was not made with the intention of halting such shooting. Parks Canada is unable to substantiate its stand because it is unable to produce documents backing its assertion.

Man, or at least his governments, has a penchant for making laws and then ignoring them. Poaching is rampant in parts of Africa, encouraged by the opulence behind the markets in the Far East. Certain countries, with Russia and Japan heading the list, impede all attempts to stop, or at least reduce, the slaughter of whales. And while reports are conflicting, Canada's acquiescence in the slaughter of harp seals is a very similar case. Game laws are openly flouted in Canada and the United States, while the Lebanese have decimated the birds of their land because they enjoy eating them (songbirds are delicacies in their estimation), or use them for target practice, raptors being especially favored.

Before looking further into the lives of these raptors, let it be understood that I considered referring to the many abuses of wild life and environment now receiving judicial appraisal, the disputants being such august bodies as Sierra Club, National Wildlife Federation, National Audubon Society, International Council for Bird Preservation, Defenders of Wildlife, Canadian Nature Federation and many others, for the list is endless. I decided against it because some cases at present in litigation may be ancient history by the time this book appears, although many seem to have a life everlasting. There was also the suspicion that, in a few instances, what I have read is but the biased opinion of the complainant. The succinctly expressed view of the defendant just might sway me the other way. In any event, the spate of such legal cases suggests that others will be along to replace those on which judgment has been brought down, so that some form of environment dispute will continue to be in the public eye. There has been, however, one recent case directly concerning raptors that should be mentioned. It stems in part, from the general interpretation of the word predator, a "definition" of which appeared in a pamphlet published by the Missouri Department of Conservation: "A predator is any creature that has beaten you to another creature you wanted yourself."

In 1977, several Texans were found guilty of shooting eagles, both golden and bald, from helicopters. This flagrant violation of the laws of their state and country had its genesis in the conviction of many Texans that eagles (and coyotes) are the principal factors behind abnormally high lamb mortality, a theory disputed by biologists. The real reason may be somewhere in between, as the golden eagle is capable of attacking lambs as well as the young of similar wild ungulates. But there is also evidence that, because of the bird's taste for carrion, the carcass it has been surprised at may not have died from an eagle attack.

The most distressing part of the various accounts of the investigation and subsequent trial was the ignorance expressed by Texas ranchers. The Texans involved exhibited a myopic approach not in keeping with the scholastic attainments of some of them. The extreme wealth of others undoubtedly swayed the thinking of those with less money. It is the despotism born of wealth that has led residents of the same state, so it is said, to hire planes to drive waterfowl toward their hidden guns.

The trial also exposed corruption by officials at almost every level of government. The display of stupidity and arrogance in this infamous case does call to mind the inability of those in power to see where they are headed; and the inability of naturalists to agree that they cannot have their cake and eat it too. There must be agreement from all levels of society on conservation and preservation if we are not to return to the horse-and-buggy days.

The autocracy of political bodies and the reluctance of departments to consult with, or work with a related one means various departments on the same or different levels of government are on a perpetual collision course, which gets us nowhere in conservation.

Their actions and statements as well as those of private individuals recall the ancient bucolic who, when asked why he had shot a pelican that had ventured far from its normal range, replied: "Because I never seen such a damn thing before."

Let us not be so obtuse. Rather, let us see both sides of the issue with equal clarity and therefore mine *some* of the resources, preserve *some* of the habitat and therefore *some* of its wildlife – including the raptors.

The Diurnal Raptors

The Diurnal Raptors

The living diurnal raptors, all of which are included in the order *Falconiformes* and are commonly and collectively called hawks, number 270, 274, 279, 287, 289 and almost any number in between. The disparity in numbers reflects the inability of ornithological authorities to agree on the validity of certain forms, one stating that a particular bird is distinct from all others and should be accorded specific status, another disagreeing, opining it is merely a variant induced by differences wrought by geography. The criterion in such cases is the ability of the two forms to mate and procreate fertile offspring. The difficulty in bringing together these questionably distinct forms to test the theory is too tremendous to contemplate. So, the layman stands aside while ornithologists of repute battle among themselves.

Of greater certainty is the distribution of these raptors, which is world-wide except for the Antarctic continent and the smaller, more isolated islands that dot the oceans of the world.

Of the thirty-nine species occurring in North America north of Mexico, thirty-eight have been reported from the lower States and twenty-three from Canada. The thirty-ninth species, Steller's sea eagle, has occurred in Alaska. It seems best to ignore an old (1901) sight record of the roadside hawk in Texas. This book treats only the sixteen, those species with which the collaborators are most familiar. Happily, the sixteen reside in or visit at some season the more populous areas of the continent. A few of these sixteen have one or more subspecific variants in other parts of the continent or in the Old World, again with the experts differing in opinion. The bird known almost throughout North America as the red-tailed hawk is subject to such variation in plumage that the scientists have encountered difficulty in defining the various sub-species, some of which, in the past, were given specific rank. Over its range, the subtle differences in habits indicate the kinds of habitat and food available, but it is, quite obviously, a single, wide-ranging species, and is the buteo of North America as the common buzzard is of the Old World. There are a few other analogues found in the Old World. Sharp-shinned hawk/sparrow hawk (not to be confused with the American kestrel); American kestrel/common kestrel; prairie falcon/lanner falcon; and, to a lesser degree, bald eagle/white-tailed eagle.

The American vultures, an all-American team of scavengers, are grouped in a suborder of their own, distinct from all other rapacious birds colloquially called hawks. Neither do our vultures include those of the Old World, all of which are components of the suborder of true hawks. The affinities of American vultures are suspect, with some authorities believing they are more closely related to the cranes, a belief not without some justification. Hawks, in general, are born blind and are surprisingly helpless for some time, unlike the precocious young of cranes, which will follow parents when a day old. American vultures hatch with open eyes and almost immediately head for the throat of their parents, seeking regurgitated food. Groups of vultures also perform a ritual reminiscent of the "dance" of cranes. The secretary bird of Africa, a unique specimen included in the true hawks, is crane-like in many respects and is thought to be related to the seriemas, themselves members of the crane order. Perhaps American vultures and secretary birds separated from a crane-like ancestor well before the Lower Eocene of as much as seventy million years ago, in which their earliest fossils have been found.

Although the American vultures have been around longer than any other group of raptors, they are not as accomplished as a distant kin, the Egyptian vulture, a member of the Old World group and centered in the country giving the bird its name. This vulture has learned to break ostrich eggs by throwing or dropping rocks on them, the only bird known to scramble an egg.

Very few of the diurnal raptors have adapted to a life under constant wintery conditions and most migrate to more equitable climes at that season. Some species make but a token withdrawal, leaving a few hardy individuals as *locum tenens*. Others are not happy until they have travelled as far as the pampas of Argentina or, in the case of Eurasian species, the southern portion of South Africa. In general, hawks of the northern hemisphere tend to move south toward, but not across, the equator.

Both ancient peoples and the modern birder have been intensely interested in bird migration, the latter being so preoccupied as to forego regular eating habits in May. Modern birding has added a new facet to the study of bird movement — the observation of the flow and numbers of hawks passing over some point of land in spring (usually April) and fall (September, or in some places, October). Hawks tend to fly over terrain that offers the best soaring conditions and therefore follow ridges from which rise columns of warm air, called thermals, upon which they float. The same conditions and thermals are sought by glider enthusiasts. When thermals (which may also rise from certain types of flat terrain) are favorable and habitual winds have pushed the hawks to a shore- or coast-line, they move along it in a narrow belt rather than challenge the uncertainty of a water crossing. But, cross water they must, just as they must pass over mountain ranges. Thus, concentrations of migrating hawks may be seen at Point Pelee, Hawk Mountain, Duluth and Cape May in Ontario, Pennsylvania, Minnesota and New Jersey respectively. Lesser points are Derby Hill on Lake Ontario, (near the town of Mexico, New York), the Outer Banks of North Carolina and the Ontario town of Grimsby, at the west end of Lake Ontario. A study of maps will show the crossings are effected at the narrowest points of water.

The shoreline of ancient Lake Iroquois, which rises abruptly in north Toronto, Ontario, is also a recognized path. Working one day in an office at the base of this escarpment, my associates were at a loss to understand my lack of concentration. Hawks of many species were disrupting my thoughts as they passed by the window throughout what was supposed to be my working day. During my eight-year residence on Sunnylea Avenue, near the southwest corner of what is now Metropolitan Toronto, I saw small but definite flights follow the street each fall. I can only assume that some topographical feature, long obliterated, gave birth to the flight-path. The flying birds were passing over a level area devoted to market gardening which, with a gradual transition, became large-scale farming to the west, the whole being a mile north of the shore of Lake Ontario. My present home is four miles to the west, in a similar area, but has yielded only stray hawks.

Because hawks have virtually no enemies other than larger hawks and man, they feel free to migrate by day and not under cover of darkness, a subterfuge adopted by most of our song birds in their endeavor to avoid enemies. Those foes small birds meet while resting and feeding are, hopefully evaded in their habitual fashion, evasion they could not hope to duplicate were they to spend the hours of daylight awing. But as the migratory flight of hawks is scarcely different to their mode of hunting, they travel as do the swallows, searching for food, all the while following their course to their southern wintering grounds or northern breeding range.

Many of our small birds are faithful to specific migration dates; and the movement of many of our hawks is, to a great extent, tied to the pendulum swing of land, shore and/or water birds. But since the raptors move only by day, their appearance in numbers, especially in fall (they are far more scattered in spring), is greatly influenced by daytime atmospheric conditions. And again, more so than the small birds whose migration front is wider and whose presence may be noted in a garden plot, the diurnal raptors are more inclined to pass over a narrowly defined area.

At my summer home near Huntsville, Ontario, I have seen evidence of red-shoulder movement as early as mid-August, with the two accipiters and peregrine following two weeks later. The broad-wing, a more common summer resident there than any other hawk, has given me no indication of massing; but the red-tail and bald eagle are on the move in the second week of September, about which time the movement of Cooper's and sharp-shinned hawks ceases. Small birds are noticeably absent at that time as well. The red-shoulder seems to be gone by mid-September, with bald eagles and peregrines replaced by rough-legs in the first week of October. Red-tails may linger into November.

From my records alone, it is difficult to assess true migratory movement about either of my homes. My figures will reflect hawk concentrations which does not necessarily include movement. But, other than the red-tail, red-shoulder, rough-leg and harrier, all hawks are moving through the Toronto region in the second week of September, the exceptions noted doing so in the third week. Except for tardy red-tails and red-shoulders, which seem to be still moving in early November, the third week of October sees the end of hawk movement at Toronto. Again, using my records only as a criterion, this marks the time of hawk concentration on Lake Erie shores.

While travelling in eastern Manitoba and western Ontario in the second week of September, 1979, I was quite aware of hawk movement, observing everything except peregrines and bald eagles. Watchers at Duluth, Minnesota, were doubtless as amazed as I at the sight of three golden eagles, a western and a Harlan's red-tail travelling in tandem, and an inordinately large number of merlins, one of which made such a fast swoop on ducks and shorebirds near Winnipeg, Manitoba, that it must have arrived at Duluth, the direction in which it was headed, five minutes later.

Hawk Mountain, near Drehersville, Pennsylvania, is part of the Kittatinny Ridge, and is one of the world's greatest vantage points for hawk-watching, the birds passing at or near eye-level. The vanguard of most species can be seen there in August. The two small bird hawks, red-tail, broad-wing, harrier, kestrel, osprey and bald eagle fight conflicting air currents over the ridge all through September and most of October. The broad-wing, osprey and kestrel close their shows in early October, but the others carry on into November, by which time the number and variety is augmented by red-shoulders, turkey vultures and golden eagles, with rough-leg replacing the broad-wing in mid-October. There is no notable period for peregrines, merlins and goshawks, the three going over in scattered fashion. The first peregrines are noted in August, the other two in mid-September. Five-figure numbers for a season and a thousand for a day are commonplace for most species.

Nor can Cape May, New Jersey, be overlooked. Sharp-shins especially, but others with a taste for passerines that have been moving down the dwindling greenery of the Atlantic coast, gather there in fantastic numbers about the same time they pass over Hawk Mountain.

In summation, it would seem that the autumn passage of the diurnal raptors is so swift that concentrations, if any, strike all vantage points at about the same time.

Hunting while high above prey implies exceptional eyesight, a sense greatly developed in hawks. Like the flycatchers, whose need for sharp vision is just as great, hawks have two depressions (fovae) in each eye, giving them far greater and clearer perception than possessed by other vertebrates, which have but one. In addition, special muscles contribute to the rapid eye adjustment required during the hawk's dive on its prey, as the slightest miscalculation can mean either continued hunger or the demise of the wrong individual. A bony process above the eye shields it from the frenzied threshing of insecurely held victims and also offers some protection when the hawk impetuously follows its quarry into brush, a habit largely restricted to the accipiters. It is this shield, which is not present in all species, that imparts such a fierce, piercing expression to the birds. A gentler mien will be found in those hawks subsisting on insects. Vultures, who fear no reprisal from their food of carrion, also lack the processes. The large, globose eyes of hawks can turn in their sockets, but so little that to follow objects, the birds will turn the head, owl-like, even, like them, viewing an object upside-down.

The sense of smell is lost in all birds except some of the New World vultures, which can locate carrion, in part, by its odor.

Hearing is no better developed in hawks than in other birds, owls excepted, and plays little part in the hunt. However, two groups have developed improved hearing to supplement sharp vision. Forest falcons and harriers have facial ruffs and bigger than average ear apertures. Although not approaching those of owls in size or efficacy, their purpose is the same—to capture a greater amount of sound. The ruff, directing sound into the ear, suggests the close relationship of these two species to the owls but is just one more case of parallel evolution. The first group, the forest falcons, inhabits the gloomy forests of South and Central America, where the superiority of hearing over vision is advantageous. The second group hunts close to the ground, where vision may, at times, be so veiled by grass and low bushes that prey is located by ear rather than by eye.

The actual capture of the prey is effected by the feet, their sharp talons piercing to the very vitals, quickly putting a victim out of commission. It is this dangerous apparatus that obliges falconers to wear heavy gauntlets when handling their charges, because the gripping is a reflex action that is also evident when any bird settles on a perch. Vultures, which are not given to killing, use their feet to hold down a carcass during their tugging rather than to administer the *coup de grâce*. The osprey can change the position of its outer toe and switch from the three-forward, one-aft aspect, common to most birds, to the ice-tong formation of woodpeckers and some others. Such adjustment enables it to carry its slippery piscine prey more securely and also prevents it from flapping around in flight.

The bills of hawks and owls are strongly hooked, the better to render their prey of flesh. Formidable as they appear, they are little used in defence and present no danger to an inquisitive person. The bill is set in a soft cere in which the nostrils open and, in the diurnal raptors, is often yellow, with some possible value in sexual and other displays. Falcons have a notched bill used to sever the spinal cord of their prey.

It is the flight of birds, especially hawks, whether migrating or hunting, that has excited man throughout his history, culminating in his development of practicable flying machines during the last 0.01 per cent of his existence in time. It would seem that inspiration for the design came from those diurnal raptors specializing in soaring or gliding, which, however, is not the only style used within the order. Other members practise flapping, diving and high-speed flight. While speed is the specialty of the falcons, and tortuous flight the trademark of an accipiter hot on his quarry, the latter do not have that flight manner patented. Despite its length of seventy-five centimetres and two-metre wing span, the crowned eagle will thread the African forest with the ease of a swallow. But the flight manner of the *Falconiformes* as a whole is so diverse that no common denominator can be used as an aid to identification as in the grouse, pigeons, woodpeckers, *et al.*

During the flight of a bird, air flows over and under the curved portion of the wing. But as the upper, convex surface is longer than the lower, concave one, it takes a longer time for an air-particle to reach a point on the upper surface than it does a corresponding point on the lower. Therefore, the air above is spread out, or thinner, while that below is massed and heavier. With the greater air pressure below, the bird is forced upward. When the two currents or masses rejoin, there is a whirling or turbulence, such as may be seen from the dust swirling at the rear or a large, speeding vehicle.

Raptors given to soaring have the outer primaries notched, the width of the feather becoming abruptly narrower toward the tip. When the bird is flying downwind or not soaring, the wing tips are closed; but when the wing is extended to soar, the primaries are spread like the fingers of a hand and are farther apart than they would be otherwise because of this notching which is sometimes very deep. The resultant space between feather tips permits air currents to slip from below to above, decreasing the turbulence described above. In addition, each feather is manipulated individually to adjust to varying currents. As modification of the secondaries is not unusual in soaring birds of any kind, it is not surprising that the California condor possesses twenty instead of the customary ten. The tail of the soarers is short and broad, capable of being fanned in flight. Yet, other modifications of wings enable the almost tail-less bateleur eagle and the long-tailed bearded vulture or lammergeir to soar just as well. These two Old World species demonstrate that nature has more than one solution.

Some diurnal raptors soar with the wings held at an angle, a shallow v or dihedral, such as is found in modern airplanes. The most pronounced angle of wings is that of the turkey vulture, enabling an observer to identify one at considerable distances. The harriers, including our marsh hawk, plane in similar fashion, but close to the ground and in a shallower v. The zone-tailed hawk of south-west United States and Mexico not only mimics the vulture's flight to perfection, but flies regularly with them, picking up live prey which, conditioned to the overhead flight-pattern of the carrion eater, pays the hawk no heed. Swainson's hawk, a buteo of the western plains of North America, flies in similar fashion, greatly confusing this writer, an easterner, when studying prairie birds. The dihedral may have been "adopted" (an incorrect term, it is true) for the same purpose as used by the zone-tail but it does not serve that purpose in the lives of those Swainson's hawks that live far north of the range of the turkey vulture.

The flesh-devouring hawks would be rather messy eaters were it not for certain adaptations. There are no feathers on the cere nor, in many cases, about the base of the bill, including the lores (the space in front of the eyes). Meat-eating hawks can therefore avoid soiling their feathers on gory food. This adaptation is carried to the extreme in the vultures, both Old and New World species having the head and neck bare. They are thus able to reach well within a carcass without smearing head feathers. But the honey-buzzard leans the other way and has short, stiff feathers on the lores to protect it from the stings of the wasps which provide it with its meals.

The diurnal raptors do not have the cryptic feathering of the owls but are still of subdued coloration, with shades of brown and buff predominating. Blue, verging on gray, and red, shaded with brown (or brown with a reddish cast) are popular, the former in the upper parts, the latter in the tail but sometimes also on the thighs and/or breast. The swallow-tailed kite of Central and South America and the south-east corner of the United States, is a beautiful bird relying only on steel blue (above) and white (below) to provide its colorful distinction. Except in a few species, such as the kestrels and some harriers, it is difficult to distinguish the sex by the feathering. Crests and long, colored thigh feathers, both used in various displays, are found in a number of tropical and near-tropical forms.

Most confusing to expert and tyro alike is the great individual variation in certain groups of *Falconiformes*. One such group is the almost world-wide genus *Buteo*, well represented in North America, where most members have not only a dark phase as opposed to a light, so-called normal one, but include an infinite variety of intermediate phases as well. Here, too, the rufous shade is usually restricted to the tail, but will vary from a bright reddish to a very pale whitish containing, perhaps, just a hint of pink.

In the raptors and the equally predatory mammals, there is a tendency for the female to be the larger. In the owls, the disparity in size is most apparent in the larger species, becoming decreasingly noticeable as one progresses from the large owls to the small ones, where equality in size is the rule. In hawks, the difference in size between the male and female is most apparent in those species whose victims can put up a struggle, whether in defence, or to escape. The victims' large size can also mean longer and more violent death-throes. Both sexes of such kinds of hawks must have an aggressive nature in order to pursue and subdue their prey. But if the male hawk was the same size as the female, his added male aggressiveness might make pair formation and mating too difficult. To bring the aggressiveness into "sexual balance," the female is therefore the larger, her aggressiveness then equalling that of her mate because of her greater size.

As it has been established that lifetime pairing is the vogue among the larger hawks, such as the eagles, it is reasoned that most *Falconiformes* pair for life. But even they, along with unmated pairs, will engage in courtship displays as they drift northward in spring, with the full ritualistic flight-display taking place when the nest site is reached.

The courtship display in most birds very often reveals hitherto concealed feathers. Thus, the peacock spreads its tail (actually, the upper tail-coverts) and the bittern will show plumes few people thought it possessed. Not many raptors are so endowed, their courtship consisting instead of shows of strength, or of speed and versatility in the air. Displays of this kind range from soaring and calling over and about the nest site to more spectacular feats such as diving from a height, with the bird flattening out at ground level and then rising sharply to repeat the performance. Some species make these frightening descents in good order but have to flap heavily to regain the original altitude of up to 300 metres, while most call loudly at some time during the display. Some Old World vultures soar in pairs, in such tight union that the wing-tips almost touch. In the usual form of paired display by hawks, the couple will soar over their territory, the male the higher, both calling the while. Then the male will dive on the female, who will roll over to fly, briefly, upside down, while presenting her talons to his. The bald eagle is one of the several species where the union of talons is actually consummated, the pair then cartwheeling until lost altitude forces a separation, whereupon they will rise to repeat the manoeuver reminiscent of those given under the Big Top. Sometimes the male will dive on the perched female for, presumably, the same reason little boys threaten to push little girls into the pond. All species also have other kinds of displays used by the female to solicit feeding or copulation.

Territory is that area within its restricted habitat where a bird, mammal, fish or frog can maintain itself and, if and when applicable, its young. A brood of clamoring robins with insatiable appetites requires that its parents gather food close to the nest and not waste time in unnecessary flight. To ensure such efficiency, the pair will "stake out" a likely area (usually accomplished by the male), nest within it (but not necessarily in its geometric center) and drive away other robins from the premises.

Diurnal raptors are not so strongly territorial as robins and some other groups of birds. Moreover, there is a wide variation in the vigor of defence of a territory from one species to another and even within a species. They also have two territories, the nest area which may be quite small, and the home range which may be many hectares in area. The larger the bird, the larger its home range and the less likely it will be to attack other, or even the same species entering its domain. Open-country raptors will have a larger home range than sylvan dwellers.

Many of the small birds, such as the robin, will winter in flocks, moving about nomadically and showing no inclination to defend any territory beyond the reach of the bill. Many of the northern raptors maintain a third territory when in their winter quarters, although its defence may be minuscule. The greater tendency is to spread out over its hunting habitat even if the species is inclined to nightly communal roosts. During winter in southern Canada and the northern United States, two red-tailed hawks will be seen in the same tree (indicative of life-long pairing). A rough-legged hawk may enjoy the same roost with impunity, just as two rough-legs will admit a red-tail to their group. A kestrel, however, may object to the presence of another raptor of any size, nor will it always tolerate large birds such as crows, ravens and great blue herons.

A male robin will announce its claim to a nesting territory by singing from a commanding perch located within it. He is also advertising he is ready to mate. Other species, both in and apart from the "song-bird" group, adopt similar measures, although the announcement may be far from musical. The diurnal raptors are not song birds, nor do they attempt to masquerade as such. But the male of the several species of chanting goshawks of Africa will repeat its melodious whistle from some perch much as does the robin, although it will be already paired. And the laughing falcon, of the tropical forests of Mexico and Central and South America, as well as our own Cooper's hawk, will give what it may consider a song – the falcon's a vesper, the hawk's, a matin, and each will sometimes be joined by its mate in a duet. It is remarkable that the raptors, so capable of inflicting fatal injuries among themselves, rarely if ever resort to physical strife, abiding instead by some protocol known to them alone.

Their lengthy breeding season requires them to start nesting as soon as they arrive on the home range; or, if non-migratory, such as the vultures and kites that remain in the south, a little in advance of the same or similar species that breed to the north of them. Preparations are simple among the falcons and their close relatives, and the vultures, as no nest is made. In the first group, what may seem to be a nest is nothing more than the mixture of the debris to be found on cliff ledges and within holes plus accumulated garbage reminiscent of an Indian kitchen midden. Accipiters, kites, some eagles, the osprey and the falcons that do not nest in holes sometimes use the old nest of another bird as the foundation of their own, adding material to their own taste. The larger falcons may eject the rightful owner, perhaps a buteonine hawk or a corvid.

Most raptors nest in trees on a horizontal limb or two, close to the trunk, but cliff ledges, rock fissures and tree cavities are also used. The harriers invariably nest on the ground, a location rarely chosen except by a few species outside North America. Where trees, and consequently old tree nests, are in short supply, habitual tree users will resort to cliff- or ground-sites. Both the American and the Old World common kestrel will use suitable nest boxes erected for them, while a discarded wagon wheel mounted on a pole will soon be topped by an osprey's nest. Recently, bald eagles in Michigan have been nesting on platforms erected for ospreys. These rest on steel legs and have anti-raccoon shields.

The males of the diurnal raptors rarely, if ever, take part in the actual nest construction, but will bring material ranging from a little to much too much. In our latitude, where the repeated use of nests is the rule, the structure is repaired rather quickly. It is this repair work and consequent addition of new material of sticks and twigs that adds to the bulk of the nest of a hawk, eagle or osprey. Some species, notably the buteos, the golden eagle and the osprey, have more than one nest, using each in rotation from year to year. Any one of these may be abandoned forever if breeding therein is not successful.

A great variety of materials has been found in the nests of birds, from cellophane wrappers to pieces of newspaper imprinted with "For Sale," but only the nest-building diurnal raptors incorporate sprigs of leafy vegetation. If such a spray is not available, grass or reeds will be substituted. This decorative touch is added throughout the nesting season, the addition falling off as incubation advances. After the eggs hatch and the young have grown sufficiently to give the female a little more freedom, she will recommence her decorating. It has been postulated that the vegetation is to shade the young, to improve nest sanitation, to prevent insect infestation and to merely make home more attractive. But none of these theories, especially the last, seems tenable. The habit does, however, tell the human observer that the nest is occupied.

The raptors, both diurnal and nocturnal, have time to raise only one brood per year. It is such a lengthy process that in two of the largest American birds, the Andean and the California condors, nesting takes place only in alternate years.

About one-third of the diurnal raptors lay two or three eggs, one-fifth of them, three or four. The rest lay only one, one or two, or four or more. In general, the larger the bird the fewer number of eggs it lays, the exception being the harriers which to compensate for the hazards of ground nesting have clutches of from two to eight, and exceptionally, twelve.

The eggs of the *Falconiformes* are large for the size of the bird and are rounded oval in shape, although some eggs are nearly round and a few quite pointed. The colors of all except those of the falcons vary from white through bluish white to greenish white, and are either unmarked, or spotted, blotched or scrawled with shades of brown, red or gray, such markings sometimes wreathing one end. There is much variation within a species. The ground color of falcons' eggs is buff or white, but so obscured by the heavy red clouding or spotting it is difficult to determine the basic shade.

Candling the eggs of a diurnal raptor reveals the relationship of the bird. The inside of the shell of the eggs of American vultures is yellowish or yellowish white; that of the falcons and caracaras, buffy or reddish; while all others show greenish.

As the eggs are laid more than a day apart, the last egg in the large clutches of harriers and the smaller hawks and falcons is laid as much as two weeks after the first. Species laying small clutches begin incubating with the (usually) first egg. In large clutches, incubation begins before the third egg is laid. In any event, the result is a nest full of young in various stages of development. The one exception is the goshawk, whose young hatch almost simultaneously due to delayed and inadequate incubation.

In both the *Falconiformes* and the owls, the female, almost entirely, incubates the eggs and, she is fed on, or near the nest by her mate. In the diurnal raptors, the male will usually call the female off the nest to some habitual perch, where the food will be passed to her. But the male harrier, after alerting his mate, will drop the food from above to the female who makes a neat catch while flying on her back.

The eggs of a robin hatch in thirteen or fourteen days, a speedy process in order to get the young into safer havens. The thirty-centimetre red-footed falcon, only five centimetres longer than the robin, incubates for the shortest time among the *Falconiformes*, a period involving twenty-two or twenty-three days. The largest of the American vultures, the condors, require close to two months. In all *Falconiformes*, the female is inclined to sit so tightly on the nest that even if it is garlanded with green, the nest appears empty.

The young are born covered sparsely with down and are very feeble, with heads so large they cannot be raised; and the eyes, while open, seem incapable of sight, much like those of a newborn infant. The young are not force-fed, as is a young robin, but go without food for a day or two, gaining sufficient strength to be able to take very small bits of meat from the bill of the parent. A point to remember when caring for a young bird orphan is that while food must be shoved well down the throat of a young robin it may be merely held on some kind of pointed stick for a hawk.

There is some evidence that the ferruginous hawk of the North American prairies caches food, sectioning it neatly in the size in which it is fed to the young, and storing it in tunnel-like passages in sage brush and grass.

A thicker, almost woolly down, soon replaces the initial covering, enabling the young bird to better survive the ordeal of rain or cold if left unattended. Feathering follows, first on the wings and tail, then the body. Now the bird can move about, at least sufficiently to back to the edge of the nest and squirt excrement well over the side, thus whitewashing the area below. The excrement is propelled with such force that the young may not only recoil, but may even perform a somersault. The amount of spattering can be used to judge the age of the young, presuming the nest is unattainable, taking into account however, the duration and severity of any wet weather preceding.

As they grow, the young spend longer periods by themselves, when they will play with loose sticks and intently eye moving objects, such as nearby flying or crawling insects, mammals on the ground and distant birds in the air. One young osprey I was watching in its nest near Banff, Alberta, was quite absorbed in the trains that passed close by the nest-tree.

The young bird solicits food from the parent until amost or quite fully feathered, by which time it will have learned to feed itself by making mock attacks on unconsumed food lying in the nest. Now, in a remarkable change in attitude, it will threaten an adult bringing food, snatching it from the parental bill and mantling its meal with spread wings. After such an unfilial exhibition, the adult will quit the scene promptly and almost in alarm.

An increasing amount of exercise in the form of wing-flapping and bouncing follows, until, some day, the young bird will attempt a clumsy flight on its own. If it can physically do so, it may return to the nest, or at least to the nest-tree, between excursions. All this is quite different to the behavior of a young robin which, unless startled from its birth place, must be enticed out by its parents, thus encouraging it to fly. Then, once out, it never returns to the nest.

The fledging period of the diurnal raptors is long, from three weeks for small species to three months in the case of tropical eagles. Obviously, the whole nest-cycle must be completed in time to get all young, particularly those of the more northern species, on the wing before the winter season.

The young of those diurnal raptors blessed with many siblings somehow avoid the strife of those hawks whose broods are low in number. The young of hawks that lay but two or three eggs engage in what is referred to as "Cain and Abel battles." The older and therefore larger and stronger bird will attack a sibling until it is killed, although a few weaklings manage to struggle out of the nest to escape torment, only to succumb to starvation in the end. The strife is ignored by the mother bird nor does she show concern when the larger of the young birds prevents the weaker from seeking shelter under the brooding hen. When the bird dies in the nest it becomes a meal for either the remaining young one or its mother. Even when the youngest survives such a grisly fate, it may starve, unable to command sufficient attention to be fed its share of food. Only when the food supply is ample and its larger sibling sated as a result, will it receive enough to eat. A hawk population is therefore regulated by its food supply.

Human foster parents may be dismayed by the incidence of myiasis in their charges, although the true parents let nature run its course. An exquisitely beautiful blue fly will lay its eggs in the ear-opening of a nestling hawk and these, hatching into maggots, crawl further into the ear, sucking blood. The health of the young bird seems unaffected. I was somewhat aghast to enter my son's room to find him, forceps in hand, calmly extracting such crawlers from the ear of a captive broad-winged hawk.

Birds in the lower orders surrender nests to man without protest. Song birds, in the higher echelon, will not attack but will raise such a clamor that what was a carefully guarded secret is one no longer. Hawks and owls will attack, sometimes to the point of drawing blood, but no definite rule can be drawn. Suffice it to say that anyone who dares to approach a hawk's nest may find himself under vicious attack from one or both parents. On the other hand, the birds may steal away so quietly he may not see them go.

If he does manage to reach the nest, he may be confronted by a young bird ready to defend itself with talons sharper and more devastating than any lancet carried in a doctor's surgical case. During the threat display, used even by adult birds in some cases, the bird leans back on its tail with wings widely spread, ready to fence with one or both feet. Sometimes the threat will be from a supine position.

Apart from the scavenging raptors, almost all of the rest of the order respond to excitement, such as brought on by nest-intrusion, with a high-pitched, repetitive "ki-ki-ki" in varying degrees of intensity and harshness. A scream, invariably described as fierce, is emitted by most larger species, particularly those addicted to preying on mammals. Predaceous mammals will scream before attacking or pouncing, startling their prey into frozen immobility for that appreciable instant that gives the predator a time-advantage. But the scream of a hawk does not seem to be used for that purpose, carrying more the hint of displeasure or the frustration of a thwarted attack. However, it must have some survival value as the vocalizations of both the Old and New World vultures, who are not killers, consists only of grunts and hisses, while the vocabulary of some of the former extends to squeals and cackles.

Those species studied around the nest suggest that all members of the order have a variety of croons, chuckles, clucks, etc., much as is heard from a domestic fowl. It is easy to attach an anthropomorphic significance to such sounds, but the calls may not stem from mother love so much as to provide a base for contrast. They will have a soothing effect on the young, assuring that all is well, but the difference between such notes and the sharp call signifying danger is so great that the electrifying effect of the latter will be more pronounced.

If one is attuned to nature, the presence of a hawk will be manifest by certain signs. A flock of flying grackles or starlings contracts, the mass now assuming the appearance of a black blob from outer space. They will have become aware of a hunting hawk and will have massed to confuse the raptor, who is now unable to single out a particular victim. Falcons such as merlins, however, may dive into the concentration of avian forms and emerge with dinner. At other times, bird song and calls are suddenly hushed as their owners freeze, knowing that any sound or small movement will reveal themselves to a hunting accipiter.

The pristine nature of the country required by these truly wild birds is fast disappearing. As each woodlot, field, forest, and area of wasteland is converted to yet another monument to man's industry, our flora and fauna die with it. It is therefore good to know that some men have the thoughtfulness to provide for the homeless and also see, that they have food as well. As a lasting protection to what may be the world's largest concentration of nesting hawks, 31,000 acres that are gouged by Idaho's spectacular Snake River canyon were set aside not too long ago. Realization that the nesting grounds were deficient in food induced authorities to add a surrounding half-million acres to the preserve.

The arrangement and nomenclature of the diurnal raptors follows that of Brown and Amadon. The range given is a condensed delineation of that of the AOU (1957), and is of the entire species, including all subspecies.

Turkey Vulture *(Cathartes aura)*

The southern prairie section of western Canada and south-western Ontario south to the Straits of Magellan in South America. Withdraws to near tropical areas in winter.

While the suborder of American vultures has been around for a good many years, the turkey vulture seems to be a comparative newcomer to the states and provinces bordering the lower Great Lakes. The first record for the Niagara Frontier Region was in 1884, at Buffalo. During the past seventy years, its numbers have increased greatly in that area. It was not until early in this century that the turkey vulture made a formal appearance at Toronto, Ontario. (We can discount one that strayed to Moose Factory, James Bay, in 1898; it may have originated in the Canadian prairie provinces, from where the species spread into the Rainy River – Lake-of-the-Woods region in historic times). Even yet, the species by no means common in the air over Metropolitan Toronto, although up to a dozen may be seen, during the early summer, at Milton, which is on the west periphery of the Toronto ornithological region, a thirty-mile radius circumscribed about its City Hall.

Milton lies at the base of the Niagara Escarpment, where the limestone fissures, caves and crevices offer the nesting sites this troglodyte prefers. It also utilizes hollow logs. The same escarpment, which also provides the updrafts of rising warm air essential to the bird's masterful, soaring flight, enabled this species to spread north into the Bruce Peninsula of Ontario. A sewage pond at Kimberley, in the Beaver Valley of Grey County, southeast of the Bruce, fascinates them. There, E. A. Westendorp, of Toronto, counted up to 119 crowded on the ground before he realized an accurate census was hopeless.

Subsequently, I visited this pond and while a dozen vultures wheeled about in its general vicinity, none was seen on the ground, so it could not be determined if the birds were eating human excrement (they have been known to eat the feces of hogs), or if they were just taking advantage of the drying warmth of the location as they cannot fly when wet. In their mastery of the air, they rely not only on thermals but dry feathers, so that following rains, they perch with outspread wings, "hanging" the feathers up to dry. The following summer I called my wife's attention to a bird drying out in that fashion and had difficulty convincing her she was not viewing a Boeing 747, so great was its wing spread.

From Kimberley and the Beaver Valley, and from upper Bruce County, the birds are now reconnoitering the Regional District of Muskoka, a surprising habitat as that area is quite heavily forested. I have seen several individuals in that district, one of which objected to the proximity of a soaring broad-winged hawk, an act of aggression rarely encountered in vultures.

But to really appreciate this bird, one must visit the more southern States, especially in winter, when the resident vulture population is greatly augmented by birds from the north. One February, during our drive from Dallas to Huntsville, Texas, we were soon aware that some kind of vulture, turkey or the black, which has a more southern distribution, was always in view. In their ceaseless cruising of the air, broad wings hold the birds aloft with virtually no effort. Occasionally the turkey vulture would tilt from side to side as it dueled with the vagaries of the thermals rising from the ground below. It was further distinguished by the angle of its wings which are held in a shallow V.

The birds gather to roost in some favored grove overnight, remaining there until the ground has warmed sufficiently to send columns of warm air skyward. After the early morning mists have been dissipated by the rising sun, revealing prospective meals on the ground, the birds scatter widely, each searching for some animal that has met its end. As the discoverer begins a slow, circling descent, neighboring vultures, correctly interpreting the first's behavior, begin to converge on the spot. And their action, no longer one of aimless soaring, alerts birds from still farther away. At Kinross, Ontario, where a couple of months previously we had seen an early spring arrival floating over fields still partly snow-covered, we witnessed the gathering of eleven vultures at the carcass of a woodchuck. Four were on the ground, five were preparing to land and two were trying to cover the final kilometre before the last vestige of groundhog disappeared.

Farther south, in the center of their distribution, such a gathering would have included dozens, rendering some carrion ranging in size from a snake to a horse. Or

ghoulishly standing around or perched nearby, waiting for the demise of a mired, diseased or fatally injured animal. Once assured of death, the birds dive in, with a minimum of squabbling punctuated only by grunts and soft hisses, the full extent of their vocabulary. The snake is soon despatched; the horse may last two or three days until it is reduced to a pile of clean bones. Perhaps an occasional grasshopper or venturesome field vole may be gathered up in the scavenging process. Otherwise, the birds exhibit gustatory enjoyment only over lifeless flesh, no matter how putrid. Obviously, the two young they rear, feeding on regurgitated carrion as they do, have a sense of taste far removed from that of humans.

The source of their food supply in the more northern parts of their breeding range is somewhat mysterious. Road fatalities abound, as any traveller may see. Yet I have never seen a turkey vulture at, leaving or approaching any road kill, the majority of which, in the north, are snakes, frogs and small rodents, all light enough to be carried away in the bill. Even in Texas where, at times, the roads seemed surfaced more with dead skunks than black top, vultures seemed to seek meals elsewhere, perhaps in the fields where traffic interruptions would not occur. It would be interesting to know how long they had to wait to be able to penetrate the armor of a dead armadillo we saw lying well off the road.

Young vultures are said to make interesting pets, provided they are house-broken of the habit of spewing the contents of the stomach when alarmed or threatened.

Osprey *(Pandion haliaetus)*

Summers from the tree-line south in both hemispheres. In North America, to the southern boundary of United States, Baja, California and some Caribbean islands. In Eurasia, to, generally, the large mountain ranges with an east-west declination through most of China to the islands of the eastern Pacific and Australia. Winters about ice-free waters throughout the eastern hemisphere and half-way down South America in the western one.

P ort Daniel Bay is a neat semicircle on the east side of the Province of Quebec, opening onto the Gulf of St. Lawrence about the entrance to the Bay of Chaleur. There is some sort of settlement there but of what kind, how large, whether for fishing or recreation, I have no idea. The sight of a fine osprey that ran through its entire repertoire shoved all civic interests into the background.

We spotted the bird circling and soaring at no great height above the water, just a few hundred metres off shore. It paused, began to hover, then commenced its thoroughly documented drop, striking the water feet first and quite disappearing for an appreciable moment. It reappeared, shrugged off water like a retriever and began its aerial ascent, a fish about a half metre long in its talons. The snout of its catch was pointing forward, as usual, for ospreys long ago discovered the futility of trying to fly with the tail of a fish flopping around to the fore.

While our word "plunge" is, according to the dictionary, rather all-embracing, its general use seems to be restricted to entering the water head first, such as does a loon from the surface, a gannet or brown pelican from the air, or a swimmer from a board or tower. The osprey is not, in my lexicon, a plunger, as its entry is always feet first, quite understandable when we remember that it catches its prey in the manner prescribed by all hawks – with its feet, not its bill.

A migrating osprey may be seen far from water, but when settled for summer or winter will be so close as to be considered a bird of the littoral, if that term may be used for both oceans and inland lakes. When your diet is almost exclusively fish that must be caught personally and not imported, you have little choice. But don't think that any old pond will do for the osprey. The water must contain rather slow-moving fish of reasonable size that are inclined to swim or bask near the surface; and the water must be relatively clear so that such fish may be seen from above. For those reasons, the osprey competes not at all with man's interests. It would soon rid us of carp if that fish did not muddy waters with its roiling.

There is another summer requirement that has some limitation on the distribution of this hawk that approximates the size of a small eagle. There must be near the water some trees of reasonable height and preferably dead, on which its nest of sticks may be built. Like the bald eagle, the osprey builds a new nest every year – using the old one as a foundation, resulting, in time, in a huge structure. Nor does this foundation go to waste when a pair of ospreys go to that "Great Lake in the Sky." A new couple will move right in and continue the original high-rise development.

Trees are not a prerequisite, however, provided the primary structure offers a fine support. The cross-arms of utility poles are favorite locations, as are metal pylons carrying heavy-voltage wires. Hydro-electric companies from Cape Cod to Key Largo, and from Portland, Maine to Portland, Oregon, take a dim view of this (an unintentional pun) because of the electrifying results and fires caused by short-circuiting. Flapping fish, the wide-spread wings of the birds or nest rubbish, soggy

from rains, conduct current far too well, creating damage that runs into many thousands of dollars annually. Fortunately for both osprey fanciers and users of electricity, changes in cross-arm construction and line-mounting are reducing this hazard. Some birds will even use a substitute support erected alongside the one carrying current, but most stubbornly return to the troublesome spot and will even rebuild with the material torn out by hydro linemen.

Elevation is not always sought for a nest as I have seen one that was almost on the ground. It was atop a stump or man-made structure in a marsh near Atlantic City, New Jersey. Another nest, near Delta, in eastern Ontario, was in a living, not a dead, tree not far from a lake. The water, however, could not be seen from the base of the tree.

One of the entertaining characteristics of this member of an order known for its dislike of human company is that it can be encouraged to nest near habitations by mounting a cart-wheel or other platform on a pole, thus enabling some statistically-minded enthusiast to record nesting house wrens (twelve centimetres) and ospreys (a half metre) on his property. In addition, he will have his garden full of bird song, as the bubbling of the wren will be accompanied by the several calls of the osprey which, while usually weak, are not unmusical. William Brewster, eminent ornithologist at the turn of the century, likened them to the pleasant chitter of purple martins. Nor need the garden be in the suburbs. In June of 1976 we saw no less than six of these great birds flying about a small lake within the city of Salmon Arm, British Columbia. The presence of strollers along the shore did not deter one bird from dropping to retrieve a deflated, orange beach ball floating near the surface. One drawback is that the proximity of these birds may affect television reception, as I found a high antenna at Flamingo, Florida, was a favorite lookout. But as the osprey is strictly a diurnal species, it is unlikely that prime-time programs would be affected.

While the osprey is well disposed to living amicably with humans, it can create some havoc among bird-life. I once saw one swoop down on resting gulls and ducks, sending them off in a noisy clatter. Another purloined a fish from a herring gull as nicely as it, itself, is robbed by the bald eagle.

The males of most hawks will bring food to an incubating or brooding female, usually depositing the fruits of their hunting labors a little distance away. The males of a few species assist, even occasionally, in duties about an occupied nest. But the male osprey is quite domestically inclined, giving his spouse ample nest-relief. I watched such an exchange of duties at Stone Harbor, New Jersey, and saw the male proffer a small fish on the occasion. This may have been in lieu of flowers, or may have been analogous to the human custom of tossing in a hat as a prelude to entering the home well after midnight.

Bald Eagle *(Haliaeetus leucocephalus)*

Summers from the limit of trees in Alaska and Canada south to the southern border of United States and Baja, California. Remains within this range in winter, withdrawing only from ice-bound waters.

Very few countries with a taste for making war have ignored the golden eagle. It has been incorporated into a national flag, emblem, seal, coat-of-arms and similar decorations in either stylistic form or an easily recognized reproduction of the living bird. If not revered, it was at least greatly admired for its ability to kill, which is what war is all about. But only the United States of America and certain Indian tribes of coastal British Columbia in Canada have placed the bald eagle on such a pedestal, a most inappropriate perch for this similarly-sized bird.

This eagle with the preposterous name (American eagle is preferred, as it is fully feathered except on the tarsi) has none of the martial qualities of the golden, but is, nevertheless, entitled to some perch, one divided between honor and dishonor. It is both hunter and scavenger; freebooter and successful stalker; an executioner of mammalian pests of the agriculturists and a sometime killer of valuable game birds; it is an adept fisherman as well, with a variety of techniques. It wears many hats. But none of them is a casque. Even its call rarely approaches a war cry.

In the memory of living man, few of the larger lakes and rivers of eastern North America were without a pair of nesting bald eagles. If present-day man would only go about his business, ignoring the great birds, those waters, unless depleted of fish, would once again mirror the huge structures, the biggest made by birds, used to cradle its young. For the bald eagle is not a shy bird. It views with equanimity the boats, both steamers and canoes, that thread the Gulf Islands of British Columbia. Ferry passengers always have at least one bird in sight, with the situation being compounded as one goes farther north toward, and into Alaska. Once they have become accustomed to humans moving about below the nest, they conduct their affairs as if in the center of Ellesmere Land. But abandonment of nest and territory will follow a mere hint of intrusion. Leave them strictly alone and it is quite possible to have bald eagles nesting above a cottage on some eastern lake.

In addition to nest disturbance, the bald eagle has been the ultimate victim of pesticides, so that its numbers have declined drastically as have those of the osprey and peregrine. Never again will man see dozens of bald eagles feeding on deer and bear that perished trying to shoot Niagara Falls unless he relies less on harmful pesticides and also restores the population of those mammals to what they were in frontier days. But hope glimmers anew. On one day in the winter of 1977-78, thirty-two eagles were seen feeding on fish mangled by the hydro-electric turbines on the Mongaup River in New York's Sullivan County.

The bald eagle is more a water bird than the kingfisher, almost equalling the duck. It has been seen floating on the surface, the result, perhaps, of fishing deeper than it intended. Rather than dropping from above, as does an osprey, it will swoop in a flat trajectory, much as does the prairie-loving ferruginous hawk, descending just low enough to snatch a fish with dangling talons. Over-zealous birds are known to even submerge. Bald eagles will join a number of other pelagic species decimating a school of fish from above while finny predators do the same from below. They also wade in shallows, catching fish with the dexterity of a racoon or otter. Their most infamous act is to harass an osprey until he drops his catch, the eagle deftly snagging it in mid-air. Other hawks and vultures are similarly hounded by the bird, while I have seen one pirate a herring gull on an inland lake. But not satisfied with this blemish on its escutcheon, it also feeds on dead fish cast up on shore and on the salmon thronging rivers of the west coast seeking their spawning ground upstream; or on their maggoty carcasses when their life cycle has been completed.

Waterfowls are almost as high on the bald eagle's list of food items; and again, the taste runs from living, through moribund, to dead birds. The eagle has been seen to catch ducks in flight, but the usual procedure is to harry a swimming flock until one is

ADULT

IMMATURE

separated, then to force the lone bird to dive repeatedly until exhausted. Sometimes this method exhausts the eagle as well. I saw these tactics once, but in switching back and forth between binoculars, telescope and camera, failed to see what kind of waterfowl was the victim and how the capture was accomplished. The eagle was an immature bird and seemed to lack the finesse of an adult.

In parts of the United States the bald eagle is considered an endangered species, but in certain areas of North America, its numbers seem scarcely diminished. That is especially true in Alaska and northern British Columbia and, I would say, about Lake of the Woods in Ontario. On a cruise there in 1964, twenty-five birds and six nests were seen, hardly an indication of scarcity. Ungava, in northern Quebec, is another stronghold in Canada, as is Chesapeake Bay in the eastern United States. With about one hundred pairs there in 1977, the population is only half what it was in the 1930s, but eagle-watchers will be pleased to know that, for the first time in twenty years, the year 1977 saw the number of successful nests exceed those abandoned.

One can be excused for confusing the immature bald and golden eagles, but no excuse should be accepted for calling an adult bald eagle a great blue heron! It happened this way: Many years ago, I was standing beside fellow birder Lucy McDougall scanning the fine marsh at Point Pelee, Ontario. Herons, chiefly great blues, seemed everywhere, all intent on some business that took them to every point of the compass. When still one more broad-winged bird rose from the marsh, long legs trailing behind, I mentally checked off another great blue, Lucy admitting later she had done likewise. Then I began to hastily flip over my mental file of field marks trying to determine which large heron had a white rump. The bird's take-off flattened out and then everything fell into proper perspective. We had witnessed an adult bald eagle rise from the marsh clutching a one-and one-half metre fox snake, each half of the reptile trailing like the two legs of a heron. The white rump, of course, was the eagle's tail. Mortification ensued.

Marsh Hawk *(Circus cyaneus)*

Summers south of the tree line in both hemispheres. In North America, south to Baja, California, New Mexico, Kansas and Virginia. In Eurasia, south generally to the east-west mountain spine swinging north of the northern edge of Mongolia. Winters south through Central America, the Mediterranean Sea and continental Asia, excepting India.

I t would be nice to know exactly what Lacépède had in mind when, in 1799, he proposed the now established name of *Circus* for the group of hawks called harriers. He may have been following Aristotle, who used the name, in its Greek form of *Kirkos*, for some kind of hawk. But our words, circle and circus, are derived from the Latin *circus*, which was both a circle and a quadrangle in which races were run. Our circus is an eleborate show where the acts take place either above a ring or, if in it, often proceeding just within its circumference, still another word with *circus* as its root. As the harriers do not habitually fly in circles, Aristotle's hawk must have been something else, probably a buteo.

The marsh hawk's hunting flight is distinctive. Flying under twenty metres, sometimes just clearing the tops of bushes, it crosses and recrosses any extensive land, not necessarily a marsh, that might be home to small rodents. It avoids the forest, nor is it happy where the tree growth is even sparsely scattered. Its flight is leisurely (quite slow, where vegetation is coarse and thick and prey consequently hard to see; much faster over the scattered grass of a near desert); buoyant and gull-like (the gray male can easily be mistaken for a gull), interspersed with periods of sailing, when the wings are held in a

V, but in a much shallower angle than the dihedral of the vulture. Like that species it will tilt from side to side as it contends with the vagaries of air currents.

The hawk's vacillating flight is slow enough that it can be checked the instant a victim is sighted, which is then pounced on from above. If the moment of attack is not favorable, the hawk may hover, awaiting a more propitious time. Aristotle – and Bernard Germain Étienne Lacépède, Compte de De Laville – certainly did not have its hunting flight in mind.

When migrating, it flies higher, sometimes very much so, even soaring under optimum conditions. But again, Lacépède – and Aristotle – must have been looking at a different kind of hawk.

But, in spring, the male does put on a show that may be classed as a circus. He begins climbing almost vertically until, when fifteen to twenty-five metres above the ground, he will stall, precipitating a nose-dive that may end three metres from disaster. The dive terminates in a graceful arc that sends him skyward again. This manoeuver is repeated as many as seventy-five times, and so impresses his intended (or life-long mate) that she may leave off watching him from the ground and engage in something more practical, like preening, or looking for something to eat. Nor does the feat make a greater impact when he somersaults at the apex of his climb. If it was this display that induced the name *circus* or *kirkos*, the Count – and Ari – may have been qualified observers after all. But, in view of some names, both scientific and vernacular, that have been bestowed on birds, it is surprising that "serrate" was not used somewhere, as the male's amatory flight path is definitely a saw-toothed one.

Like other hawks, the male is a good provider during the nesting season, but where most others considerately carry the food right to the female, the marsh hawk is content

MALE DORSAL VIEW

FEMALE DORSAL VIEW

to drop it from above, hoping his spouse will be alert and will leave the nest in time to intercept the offering before it touches the ground. She usually is — and does.

Just as the hawk owl seems part hawk, the marsh hawk seems part owl. The hawk's keen hearing is enhanced by a feathered facial disc as is found in the *Strigiformes*. Moreover, the marsh hawk and short-eared owl hunt over the same kind of ground for the same kind of food. Each almost never perches in a tree, resting instead on the ground, sometimes even sharing the same grassy or marshy tract. In fall and winter, marsh hawks may roost communally, but, come hunting time, each individual will hasten to its special preserve.

The marsh hawk's method of hunting is designed primarily to catch and harry (hence the alternative name of harrier) mice, voles, cotton rats and other small grass-haunting rodents, the disposal of which gives the hawk a good name. But it also catches birds, a trait that has not endeared it in certain quarters. It is my opinion that the capture of grass-haunting sparrows is more accidental than designed. Such birds can look very mouselike in their sometimes creeping movements. But, then again, some of the birds falling to the marsh hawk are larger than sparrows, birds that have no resemblance to a rodent. The common grackle is quite aware of this predilection, as I have seen a flock, on the advance of a marsh hawk, leave the reeds of a marsh for the greater security of trees. Very frequently, the harrier will also end the misery of a moribund duck that was not retrieved by a hunter.

The marsh hawk's chattering call is to be heard almost only when a potential enemy invades its nest territory which, if not in a marsh, will at least be on the ground in a wet area.

Northern Goshawk *(Accipiter gentilis)*

Found south of the tree line in both hemispheres. In North America, south to the Great Lakes and New England in the east and down the cordillera into Mexico in the west. In the eastern hemisphere, the forested regions of Europe (except Great Britain and Portugal), Russia and Japan and the northern parts of the Middle East, China and India. In North America, winters irregularly south to Texas.

The average person of today, with little interest in birds and none in going afield in search of them, will see (with, perhaps, a complete lack of perspecuity), certain of our hawks, but he will have little chance of meeting a goshawk. The name, by the way, is pronounced goss hawk and is a corruption of goose hawk, although geese are minuscule factors in its diet.

This large, bold, aggressive predator, ranked equal to, and even above the gyrfalcon by the falconers of Turkey, Persia and Mongolia, summers in the deep forest rarely traversed by man. It winters there, too, indulging only in more extensive wandering as the savagery of winter reduces its food supply. But, as two items prominent in its diet, the hare and the grouse, are subject to periodic population crashes, some, if not all goshawks just as periodically move south to greener, albeit snow-covered pastures in winter. These irruptions occur in nine- to eleven-year cycles.

In former times, the inattentive observer had a better opportunity to see this bird if he kept chickens or visited a farm, for the goshawk was the scourge of the poultry yard of old. Not even flapping arms or human screams deterred its attack. Snatching a hen from the foot of an irate farmer was a commonplace incident. Hunters of today may see a goshawk retrieve a wounded game bird before they or their dog can act; but better protection about the now-industrialized poultry farm, combined with the disappearance of the old-style barnyard with its freely roaming hens, have thwarted the hawk's depredations. But it is still an audacious bird. While other hawks will make a hurried departure at my approach, or, if directly overhead, will keep some distance up, the goshawk, along with its two relatives, is the only one to have flown at no great height over my head. It is at such times that its downy white pantaloons are quite evident. These fluffy undertail coverts are erected in prominent display during courtship flights.

When it has some distant objective, the goshawk flies high, almost invariably in a pattern of five flaps and a glide, rarely if ever soaring in even a tight circle. But when hunger transforms this Dr. Jekyll into a Mr. Hyde, the bird becomes almost falcon-like in flight and appearance. Now, on the hunt, it flies below the treetops, sometimes quite close to the ground and always seeking to surprise its prey in the typical accipiterine fashion of using a tree or bush to screen its approach. If, in its hunting, its presence has been revealed, it will turn its attention elsewhere. Or, again, it may only seem to, returning with so much greater stealth that one can only feel it is aware that its first approach was made too carelessly. Sometimes, too, it will perch quietly within a leafy tree (another reason why it is seen less frequently than, say, a red-tail), making a sudden onslaught on an unwary bird or mammal. If the prey receives some warning and heads for cover, the goshawk will follow the most tortuous of courses until the prey is seized and quickly despatched by talons resembling rapiers affixed to a vise. Even if the quarry disappears under tangled shrubbery, the hawk, undeterred, will follow on foot. There is some evidence that it will even preface some hunting with preliminary ground stalking.

At the moment of killing, it has been observed that the bird's eyes flash flaming red, an indication, perhaps, that this species is really consumed with a lust for blood. Ordinarily, with hunger appeased, it will cease hunting, but so ingrained is its instinct to kill that the appearance of more potential victims may be the catalyst to another orgy of slaughter. In this respect, its habits are almost musteline, killing with the indiscriminate, maniacal fury of a weasel.

Its fierce nature is further exhibited about the nest. There have been a few instances where the parent birds quietly disappeared when nest-areas were invaded by humans, but in the vast majority of cases, the intruders, be they man, dog or bear, were put to rout. To study the nesting habits in intimate detail requires more equipment than just climbing irons. It is hard-hat territory, with dexterity in the use of a club mandatory. In the region of my summer home a tree, containing a nest, had to be felled, and in order to do so with impunity, the tree-cutters were obliged to despatch both parents before tackling the tree.

The birds give fair warning at such times, although their piercing *kak-kak-kak*, suddenly shattering the funereal quiet of the forest, can separate a bushwacker from his epidermis. This is a good time to make a wide detour, forgetting the large but neat and well-constructed nest placed in a beech or maple and wedged into the same sort of crotch selected by a robin. But the hawk, by virtue of its greater size, uses, perforce,

ADULT

IMMATURE

only the principal one in the larger trees, selecting a spot as much as twenty-five metres up. A few nests, usually in an alder or poplar, may be as low as five metres.

A plucking and skinning post, such as a stump or old nest, may be thirty metres away from the occupied nest. Sometimes this larder, maintained mostly by the male, will be filled to capacity with carcasses nakedly arrayed in obscene display. Were it not for the absence of a sawdust-covered floor, one would feel transported back to the old-time butcher shop.

Sharp-shinned Hawk *(Accipiter striatus)*

Summers from the northern extremity of the more lightly forested regions of Alaska and Canada south throughout United States (except the Gulf States and Georgia), and Central America, along the cordillera of South America to Bolivia, Paraguay and adjacent Brazil. Winters chiefly south of Canada except for southern British Columbia.

This is the bird more deserving of the name "sparrow hawk," so mistakenly once given to the American kestrel. The sharp-shin is the American analogue of the European sparrow hawk, both members of a cosmopolitan group of accipiters whose sole mission seems to be the decimation of small birds.

Like its two larger relatives, the goshawk and Cooper's hawk, it has the typical accipiterine flight of five flaps and a short sail, but it becomes almost falcon-like in action and appearance when in pursuit of prey. At that time one must guard against confusing it with the blue-backed male merlin.

The sharp-shin avoids the leafy forest, preferring instead lightly wooded areas or abandoned fields well on the way to becoming, years hence, the climax forest typical of the region. My summer home is adjacent to land which was farmed up to the mid-forties. During the period of cultivation, the sharp-shin was unknown, although the usual unprotected flock of chickens was there for the taking, as were numerous small birds that frequented the edges of the heavy hardwood forest. The sharp-shin did not appear until twenty-five years after farming was discontinued and all of the fields were overgrown with scattered shrubs and small trees, the covering it uses to mask an approach on its quarry.

When the hawk rounds or tops a bush and meets with a possible victim, the suprise is possibly mutual, but the hawk reacts the faster, its short wings and long tail enabling it to change course instantaneously and to drop on prey not yet recovered from the sudden appearance of its foe. Not, however, that all such attacks are successful. It will miss more than 80 per cent of the time and is less inclined to follow up initial failures than are our other two accipiters. This was evident when one flew past me in the wake of a small flock of pectoral sandpipers just settling on a mudflat. The hawk missed its strike on the grounded shorebirds but kept on going and was not seen again. The attack was made within a few metres of me, so it was not my presence that halted a reprise.

As the sharp-shin preys on small songbirds, it must keep pace with their movements or starve. Thus it is that from late August through early October, when hordes of migrating small birds crowd thicket and hedge, the sharp-shin is much in evidence. In mid-September I have seen little piles of the feathers of thrushes dotting the forest floor at Point Pelee, on the Ontario shore of Lake Erie, mute evidence that the dozens of winged projectiles seen there through a single day had dined sumptuously. The flight seems less pronounced in spring, perhaps because the vernal migration is of shorter duration. Strangely, almost all the sharp-shins passing through Pelee in autumn are birds of the year. It is such birds, too, that, lacking the wisdom of maturity, take poultry and make other almost suicidal attacks when in sight of humans.

Small as it is (it ranks with the kestrel as our smallest hawk) there is as much audacity packed into the sharp-shin's body as there is in the goshawk, which is five times as heavy. It will snatch chickens and winged game from the feet of a human and attack birds many times its size. It does seem to contain its instinct to kill to that period when hunger is demanding, the appeasement of which may be accompanied by shrill squeals of excitement.

Perhaps its volubility during the butchering is because it has remained very silent during the hunt, for, like the other two accipiters, it is not a noisy bird except during the nesting season. Even then, silence is the rule, with courtship a very quiet affair. Aggressive action against intruders into its domestic affairs is accompanied by the shrill, high-pitched accipiterine cackle common to the Cooper's and the goshawks, a rapid repetition of the syllable *kek, kik, duck* or *dik*, each writer of hawks apparently having heard the call on a different wave-length. My personal preference excludes a consonant at the beginning.

This means that you have little likelihood of hearing the species unless you are near a nest, and that is not likely to occur unless you invade a field well sprinkled with clumps of small conifers, principally pine or spruce. The nest, a rather flat structure of clean sticks, will probably be on a horizontal limb (or two) against the trunk, anywhere from three to ten metres up. The birds may attack but are easily thwarted, as this is a hawk little longer or bulkier than a robin. If you are capable of fighting off mosquitoes, you will survive the nest examination unscathed.

ADULT

IMMATURE

59

A strange anomaly is that while the sharp-shin subsists almost exclusively on small birds, which become singularly still and silent if they are aware of a hunting hawk, it is not immune to attacks by its sometime prey. Both barn and tree swallows will drive it away, helped, no doubt, by the concerted action of a flock; while I have seen one put to rout by a bird a little smaller than the hawk but which was so far away I could not determine if it was a kingbird or a red-winged blackbird. Ordinarily, such species fill the bird's meat order precisely.

Cooper's Hawk (*Accipiter cooperii*)

Summers from a line connecting the tip of Vancouver Island, British Columbia, the top of Lake Superior in Ontario and the end of the Bay of Fundy in Nova Scotia south to northern Mexico. Winters south through Central America, withdrawing from all of Canada except southern British Columbia and, occasionally, southern Ontario.

A party of us were fishing for bass close to a steep slope clothed with hemlocks, behind which was the sugar maple-yellow birch forest so typical of Ontario's Muskoka Region. Our attention was diverted from piscine affairs by the dramatic appearance of two adult Cooper's hawks which shared, for a brief while, a large branch only ten metres away and almost over the shoreline. One bird flew off when discovered, but the other remained for a couple of minutes, glaring at us defiantly as if daring us to take the prey it was clutching in one yellow talon. We were unable to identify the victim other than that it was a bird, as we could see feet and bill but thought that the unfortunate creature reflected the characteristic olive-green of an ovenbird. Although the Cooper's hawk is quite non-aggressive about the nest, it has an overabiding disdain for humans, as illustrated by the foregoing example.

It is equally undeterred by the presence of people about a poultry yard or dovecote, returning in the face of brandished brooms and more lethal armaments for yet another attack. This devil-may-care attitude seems confined to immature birds, as there are several instances of Cooper's hawks nesting near poultry yards without the adults molesting any part of the flock.

Cooper's hawks fly in the usual accipiterine pattern of five flaps and a sail, and have the family trait of using trees and bushes to screen their approach, snatching a victim before it is startled into flight. If the quarry has been able to get underway, the hawk will follow it through trees with all the ease and grace of a barn swallow hawking for insects. Should the prey dive into shrubbery, the hawk, with a remarkable transition from swallow to mink, will follow with musteline tenacity. Like the goshawk and sharp-shin, the Cooper's hawk may hunt actively, in a hedge-hopping campaign, or passively, hiding within a heavily foliaged tree at the edge of woods, from which it launches an onslaught so sudden its victim may never be aware of its final moments. It has a few tricks of its own, too, such as hopping about in grass to flush quail it has heard calling. All accipiters find garden-feeding counters a good source of food but Cooper's hawks (again possibly immature birds only) can drive the keeper of such a station up a high wall.

Cooper's and sharp-shinned hawks are very competitive, the only difference in their food being one of size, as, the larger the individual, the larger the prey it can subdue. And since a male Cooper's and a female sharp-shin are about equal in dimensions, it may be appreciated that the same stretch of woods will not hold both. On migration, they are apparently seen together, but this is only because each moved in unison with the pendulum of the small-bird migration.

In the field, Cooper's hawk is distinguished from the sharp-shin chiefly by its rounded tail, but it has a few other mannerisms that make one think that the bird in question may be the larger species. While none of the accipiters makes a habit of soaring in circles, Cooper's seems to indulge in this more than the other two. One cloudless August day I puzzled over the identity of a long-tailed soaring hawk, unable to keep it in

ADULT   IMMATURE

62

view for long because of intervening treetops. Then the birds sailed right overhead, to exhibit with utmost clarity all the overhead flight pattern and markings of a Cooper's and not, as I had been trying to make myself believe, a broad-winged hawk. Cooper's is also noisier than the sharp-shin, the male serenading his mate each dawn during the period of incubation. Not infrequently, she will quit her duties to perform a duet with him for a short while. It is not a musical effort, the series of rather harsh *kluks* no more captivating than the reiterated *sip* of a chipping sparrow, and certainly nothing an aspiring composer would want to work into a woodland symphony. This hawk has a variety of calls, as do most birds, the one most frequently heard being a cackle a bit deeper than the sharp-shin's series of *kaks*. Cooper's also has a drawn-out, whistled *sweeur*.

There seems to be some discrepancy in summarized reports of its breeding. Arthus Cleveland Bent, whose *Life Histories of North American Birds* are classics, avers it uses white pine almost 60 per cent of the time; Drs. Brown and Amadon in their *Eagles Hawks and Falcons of the World* state it rarely breeds in conifers. Like the red-tailed hawk, any preference is probably dictated by the forest growth of its adopted region. When using a deciduous tree, it wedges its nest into an upright crotch; but if it selects an evergreen, it builds on one or more horizontal branches tight to the trunk. The nest is characterized, according to Bent, by containing more down than appears in a sharp-shin's. Like the other two accipiters, it has a plucking post within one hundred metres of the occupied nest. Scattered feathers about a stump, log or old nest are a clue to the presence of one of the three; the absence of aggression suggests the work is that of a Cooper's hawk.

Like most hawk species, the male hunts assiduously for the sitting female, although he seems to find incubation irksome, quitting such duty with alacrity, a not-inexcusable attitude, as much of, if not all the nest was his creation.

Red-shouldered Hawk *(Buteo lineatus)*

Except for an isolated race in coastal California and Baja, California, summers east of the Great Plains below a line connecting Sault Ste. Marie in Ontario and the end of the Bay of Fundy in New Brunswick, south along the Gulf Coast to Vera Cruz, Mexico. In winter, withdraws from north of the Great Lakes.

On the first day of one December, my wife and I, engaged in roadside birding, pulled off the highway to indulge in that great American institution — a coffee break. From the well-wooded pond that almost touched the road-shoulder on our right, a hawk rose, to fly up to a branch overlooking the water. Coffee was forgotten as we imbibed, instead, the great beauty of the bird. "A red-shoulder!" I whispered, gazing at a breast as solidly and deeply red as a robin's. No specimen or colored plate I have ever examined shows or reproduces the deep brick red displayed by that hawk. I fondly imagined it to be the subspecies found in Texas, a strikingly beautiful bird whose dark wings are more contrastingly lined with white than in the northeastern race; or even the dangerously rare western form, the so-called red-bellied hawk of California. But wisdom dictated that neither had any business being in southern Ontario, particularly on December 1, at which time very few red-shouldered hawks of any subspecies will be found in that province.

The red-shoulder lives much as does the red-tail, nesting on the edges of woods and hunting over open country. The two, while slightly more friendly than the Hatfields and McCoys, tolerate each other only because the red-shoulder is more an eater of snakes and frogs than of rodents, and therefore inclined to keep to wooded swamps and ponds rather than to the drier fields dominated by the red-tail.

While the more northern birds of this species favor wooded areas for nesting and a good deal of their hunting, the dominant race of Florida makes extensive use of that state's prairies, especially in the Kissimmee region in the geometric center of the state. Hawk-watchers there have their work made easy because of the preference of local hawks for fence-posts as lookouts. The red-shoulder of Texas finds a similar dearth of forests of large trees and, like the Florida birds, favors roadside posts. Possibly because these birds are more easily seen in those southern states, their striking wing pattern made a far greater impression on me there than it has in the north. I felt that the southern birds were approaching the startling beauty of the so-called "red-bellied hawk" of the coastal region of the Pacific states.

The red-shoulder is a hawk given to soaring, although to a slightly lesser degree than its near compatriot. Like the red-tail, it will perch for hours, on the watch for a snake, frog, mouse or shrew. During such vigil it may also be looking down on a hen yard, fully ignoring the source of the farm wife's pin money. It seems that it transgresses only when the demands of its young become too insistent. Then it may indulge in small, feathered prey of any kind.

The red-shoulder drifts north with red-tails and others of that ilk when the fleecy clouds of March sail across a sky of intense blue. As there is ample evidence that most hawks mate for life, its companion, if any, will be its mate, yet the species is not averse to sharing air currents with another couple or two or even some odd bird on the make, confirming that domestic triangles are not restricted to the human race. Its goal will be a patch of well-watered woods of beech and maple, where it or its predecessors have nested all through the memory of man. There, whether to charm its mate, to impress a replacement, as death happens here as elsewhere, or to woo its first spouse, the male will break off its soaring to dive earthward in one spine-tingling plunge, or a series of shorter ones, each platformed by more soaring. Almost all the while he will be screaming *kee-yoooo* at the top of his lungs. I watched such a performance in Toronto's Sunnybrook Park one March day, the bird ending its display with such a steep dive I expected to find its battered body on the ground ahead of me. But, before I reached that spot, it rose again, its screaming undiminished.

This is the call said to be imitated by the blue jay, but I think that call is just as natural to the jay as is the nasal one that gives it its name. There seems to be no point to the jay's imitation, nor does that bird even try to imitate any other hawk — or bird, for that matter — although a few individuals do engage in mimicry.

The red-shoulder seems to have no special liking for any particular kind of tree other than that the growth must have a well-spread crotch some distance (up to twenty metres) from the ground, a requirement that virtually rules out conifers. The flat-topped structure of sticks and twigs is almost as wide and deep as a red-tail's and may be

ADULT

IMMATURE

used repeatedly or in rotation with one or two other nests annually. The barred owl seems to complement the red-shoulder, nesting as it does in much the same kind of woods. The two may share the same nest, although not at the same time, the hawk taking over when the owl moves out.

Red-tailed, broad-winged and Swainson's hawks make conspicuous fall migrations, the latter two forming fairly tight flocks of hundreds of individuals. Their progress in spring is much less spectacular. Sometimes the drifting forms of an already mated pair are the only ones to be seen together. The red-shoulder approaches migration differently, slipping away, almost but not quite unseen, in autumn, but coming north in a scattered body in spring. The red-shoulder flight was very noticeable and protracted in 1976. Small groups seemed to be everywhere. Yet I was not conscious of an increase in their numbers in the summer months following.

The heavy migration was a hopeful sign that the red-shoulder could be recovering from low population levels. It had been approaching the status of threatened species due to undetermined causes, which probably included reduction of habitat and the wanton use of pesticides.

Broad-winged Hawk
(Buteo platypterus)

Summers south of the spruce forest (taiga) south to the Gulf of Mexico, east of the Rocky Mountains in Canada and the Gulf Plains in United States; also in many islands of the Caribbean. Winters from Florida south to northern Peru and western Brazil.

The broad-winged hawk is another of those birds whose name defies all reason. Its wings are no wider than those of other buteos, while the bird, except for certain markings, is a scaled-down version of the red-tail.

This hawk is a paradox. It spends the summer, not in a woodlot surrounded by fields, but in quite remote forests well sprinkled with swamps and boggy lakes and dotted with natural or cultivated clearings. But, after living in seclusion from April or May through September or October, it gathers in loose bands of twenty, fifty, hundreds and even thousands of individuals, and wheels in the most unconcealed fashion southward to its far distant, winter home south of the United States.

The spectacular flights (such a body of hawks is called a kettle, although history does not relate why, unless it is because the birds "boil up") begin in mid-September, when the usually few clouds are billowing along under a spanking north or northwest wind. But the flight of the hawks is very different to that of the clouds. The birds, sometimes so high as to be seen with difficulty, sometimes so low as to be easily identified without visual aids, wheel, drift and circle about on spread wings and tail. Yet, for all their aimless wandering, their direction is inexorably south. Their seemingly uncertain movement has often confused me to such a degree that I am never sure if the kettle in view is the same one seen headed "that-a-way" five or ten minutes before.

When the birds fly low, or over elevations such as at Hawk Mountain, Pennsylvania, they, at one time, ran into a fusillade that killed hundreds in the days when man's pecking order was determined by his skill with a gun. It is the bird-watcher who benefits now. Sitting or lying on some point favored by migrating hawks, his tally will be ticks on a checking-card rather than limp carcasses on a stick. And his count will include all of the hawk species, for the little broad-wing attracts other hawks during migration just as the chickadee attracts other small birds. The broad-wing sometimes comes north in the same manner, but I have seen such a flight only once, at Point Pelee, Ontario. This mode of travel is an effortless, economical way to commute between the bulge of South America and the hardwood forests of New England and Canada.

The broad-wing has a mild, inoffensive disposition. It does seek solitude in summer and winter, yet seems unaffected if you venture into its retreats. Retirement to a branch a little more distant is its only visible objection. It will return to its first perch, if that is a favorite one, while you are still in view, making it a too-tempting target to the gun-toters of summer. The beauty of one summer day was besmirched when I found the body of an immature broad-wing at the edge of a bush road. A few scattered feathers were testimonials of its death-throes, while its exposed breast, glowingly creamy amidst its streaks of fuscous, would soon attract maggots. I had only one thought for the rest of the day – why?

ADULT   IMMATURE

When on the watch at some favorite vantage point, the appearance of a frog, snake, mouse or even large insect will evoke in the broad-wing much the same quivering eagerness displayed by my Scottish terrier when a squirrel invades his premises. The lethargic lump of feathers perched overlooking a wooded swamp is transformed into a tail-twitching, body-swaying, small-eyed killer. A quick plunge, and it is over. Back on the perch, the luckless mouse or shrew is gulped head first; anything larger is neatly skinned, pulled apart and eaten piecemeal. It employs the more sedate, polished manner of an Englishman in his club than the uncouth performance of isolated aborigines. Insects may be eaten while the bird is on the wing. If the hawk were more agile, it just might consume more birds, but its leanings that way are to nestlings, a habit fortunately confined to comparatively few broad-wings. I imagine that even fewer are given to dangling a mouse while soaring over a lake. I'd like to think that this bird, which I watched for five minutes, did not favor violence but preferred to scare its victims to death by threatening to drop them to a watery end. Another broad-wing which seemed to depart from the norm was the bird that swooped in on a one-eyed, and somewhat tame grackle that had been frequenting my summer home. There are many plausible reasons for the unprovoked attack, but their enumeration would be an exercise in futility.

The broad-wing haunts much the same woods as does the eastern wood pewee, one plagiarizing the call of the other. The two calls are not as similar as the *kee-yearr* of the blue jay and red-shouldered hawk, but are very close phonetically and qualitatively. The broad-wing begins explosively before whining the principal sound, where the pewee bemoans plaintively throughout. The hawk's note peters out in a whistled hiss or squeak, the whole sounding like *pss-eee-oh.*

It is in these woodland haunts that the broad-wing builds a rather shoddy nest of sticks and twigs, lodged in a crotch of a deciduous tree or tight against the trunk on a horizontal branch of a conifer. But like the bird that dared the mouse to jump without a parachute, and the one that had a thing against one-eyed grackles, it may nest elsewhere, such as about six metres up in a yellow birch by a roadway joining my cottage to another sixty metres distant.

Red-tailed Hawk *(Buteo jamaicensis)*

Summers from near the tree limit in central Alaska and northern Canada south to Panama and most of the Caribbean islands. Winters throughout its summer range except that it withdraws from all of Canada except coastal British Columbia and southern Ontario.

Under its various guises, and it has many, and despite its equally numerous names, both scientific and vernacular, *Buteo jamaicensis* is still a "red-tailed hawk." Its tail may not have on its upper surface that beautiful shade of rufous so well known in the east, but instead may be pale almost to the point of being pure white; it may be mottled, barred, streaked or whatever. It may be called Krider's hawk or Harlan's hawk, subjects of century-old debates but both now considered subspecies of the most wide-spread hawk of North America. Perhaps the red-tailed buzzard of Chile and Argentina is also a race, long isolated from the parent stock by the vast forests of the Amazon valley. The habits of all these birds of confusing plumages and multifarious names are similar except for those differences imposed by environment. The convergence into one species by Doctors Leslie Brown and Dean Amadon renders the task of writing much easier. Those whom Brown and Amadon have lumped together let no man split asunder.

A tawny tail is favored by 24 per cent of those species Brown and Amadon include in the genus *Buteo*. Our red-tail is the only North American hawk so marked, a blessing to tyro hawk-watchers and an irritant to those experts who, in exasperation, reiterate that just because a hawk does not have a reddish tail does not mean it's some other species. Red-tails without red tails may look uncommonly like certain plumages of Swainson's, rough-legs, broad-wings and red-shoulders, sometimes confounding even hawk experts.

Although a rufous tail is not common throughout this complex species, its habits, as already stated, differ only according to its surroundings. Western red-tails thrive on prairie dogs and ground squirrels, items missing entirely from the diet of the eastern bird for the incontestable reason that such mammals do not occur in the east. Nor can the prairie-loving Krider's soar over, or nest near the edges of hardwood forests, as does the eastern form, because its home is on the more less treeless plains.

Of the four species of buteonine hawks found commonly in northeastern North America, the red-tail is the most accomplished soarer. One, according to Neltje Blanchan writing many years ago, kept to the air for nine hours commencing at seven in the morning. The effort expended in such flight is minimal, as the bird is held aloft by thermals, those columns of warm air rising from the ground below. Direction is controlled by altering the plane of the tail, which may, at times, be quite vertical; or by shifting the angle of wings, tail and body to slip sideways with increasing velocity and thus drift downward to another thermal.

At times, such soaring seems to be a manifestation of *joie de vivre*, but essentially its purpose is twofold: To migrate long distances with the least effort; and to hunt. All the while the bird is completing its wide circles, even during migration, it is scanning the ground below for signs of rodents or other small animal life. It will not plummet onto a victim but may dip to a perch to wait until the prey is off guard before swooping down to pin the victim to the ground. Small stuff is carried to an exposed limb, but large victims will be butchered and either eaten where captured, with the bird perhaps returning from time to time; or a portion will be carried to its mess hall.

When disinclined to soar or if unable to do so because of a scarcity of thermals, the red-tail will watch for an exposed lofty lookout, just as patiently awaiting the appearance of something to eat. And again, its patience will last for hours. Less frequently, it will hunt by gliding low over land, almost in the fashion of an accipiter. Occasionally, too, it may hover over a spot, no doubt awaiting the reappearance of a mouse, or holding off its descent to some more propitious moment. Never, however, have I seen a red-tail hover as long as, or with the ease of the larger rough-legged hawk.

The red-tail has still another trait endearing to hawk-watchers, especially those confused by its multiplicity of plumages. While soaring, in moments of vexation or anger, or perhaps because of sheer exuberance, it will give a shrill, high-pitched scream resembling a sound heard more frequently in the past than today. It suggests the sudden release of steam from a safety valve, its volume diminishing into a wheezing and sputtering finale as the pressure returns to the proper level.

In its hunting, the red-tail is pre-eminently an open country species. Whether

ADULT

IMMATURE

soaring at dizzying heights or perching in lofty grandeur (the ravages of Dutch elm disease created untold watchtowers for this bird), it does so only when it can scan fields, cultivated or abandoned; prairies or meadows; or wasteland not yet fully claimed by shrubbery and small trees. To nest, however, it seeks the forest; not their depths, but their edges. The kind of tree makes little difference. But whatever the nature of the woods in general, hardwood, coniferous or mixed, it insists on the tallest tree in the area, building as high as twenty-five metres up. Old, perhaps still occupied nests, may be seen on some elm surrounded by others equally dead, all looking like a somber convention of amputees suffering from infectious mononucleosis. Obviously, where tall trees are at a premium, it will build closer to earth and will nest in a saguarro when woody growth is absent.

Its ample nest, the largest of all our buteos, consists of sticks and twigs arranged in a bulky mass. The scream of the male may be the first indication that you are nearing its domicile. Then the bird itself will appear, circling ever closer as you near its nest. Finally, the female will join him. Contrary to the thesis, perhaps self-originating, that western peoples are friendlier than those of the east, it is the western red-tail that is inclined to make physical objection to your presence.

In winter in the northeast, the red-tail is, if not the most common, the most easily observed hawk. One February day, with the thermometer flirting with minus twenty degrees Celsius, my wife and I birded from the comfort of our car. We poked into all the roads dead-ending at Highway 401, west of Toronto, for a distance of twenty-five kilometres, and tallied thirty-two red-tails, but only eight rough-legs and seven kestrels.

While the red-shouldered hawk was the favorite of A. C. Bent, the red-tail is highest in my family's esteem. Any drive through open lands will be punctuated by a pleased, even proprietary announcement, as if we had something to do with its creation. "There's a red-tail!" one will say. And, if traffic permits, we will stop and crane our necks to peer at the object of our affection. High on a nude limb of some grotesque skeleton of a dead elm, the red-tail will regard us with regal disdain, its symbol of office, a chain, or sometimes a sash, draped low over its gleaming white front. We drive on. Our day has been made.

Rough-legged Buzzard *(Buteo lagopus)*

Summers in the treeless tundra of Europe, Asia, Alaska, Canada and the Canadian Artic archipelago. Winters south to the east-west cordillera in Eurasia and to a line connecting the ends of the Gulfs of Mexico and California in North America.

The rough-leg, the largest buteo found regularly in the east, was given scant attention by earlier authors. It is observed in settled areas of Canada and the northern United States only in winter, rarely reaching the abodes of many of the early bird historians, who therefore had little opportunity to study it.

It summers in the tundra and in the transition zones between that and the taiga, dining well on the northern lemmings. If these mouselike mammals suffer one of their periodic population crashes, the rough-leg (and a better mouse-trap has yet to be built) is forced south until it finds a more reliable food supply. This irruption occurs about every four or five years. In between times lesser numbers invade the south from southern Canada to the Gulf States and to near the Mexican border. While their tendency is to stay just south of snow-covered areas, whatever their numbers in winter, there are always a few that emulate well-to-do humans and seek areas of warm sunshine. Alexander Sprunt relates of a pair so enamored of Florida's sunshine they remained to nest at Lake Okeechobee. Unfortunately, while the hawks' description tallied with that of the rough-leg, neither Sprunt nor any other reputable ornithologist saw the birds, leaving the record in doubt.

Somewhat naturally, the birds linger everywhere mice, chiefly meadow voles, abound. Thus, the hawk is partly nomadic, moving elsewhere when some particular larder is depleted, or when even a good source is covered by too much snow. In spring, it will move north as the snow-cover disappears.

The rough-leg has been described as being of crepuscular inclination. It is, indeed, more active in failing or poor light than any other of our hawks. It is, however, just as diurnal as they but with a tendency to near-nocturnal activity. Since it is capable of remaining all winter in localities where the light is poor, it is accustomed to hunting in near-darkness, so that, when wintering in the south, it may continue its activity when other hawks have called it a day.

The rough-leg has much the same wing and tail development as the other buteos, and is, like them, an accomplished soarer; but as winter contains fewer good sailing days than summer, its flapping flight will seem habitual. On the hunt, it will flap and glide, sometimes as low as fifteen metres, above those meadows, fields or marshes harboring voles. Sighting a potential snack, it will check its progress and hover, with all the dexterity of a kestrel or kingfisher, but with wings flapping rather than vibrating. Feet will be lowered in anticipation of a pounce on some wandering mouse. If an opportunity is lost, the landing-cum-grappling gear will be retracted and the bird will resume its quartering.

Its ability to hover is puzzling, as some buteos do not seem to have mastered the art, yet the shape of all is very similar. The red-tail will hover occasionally, the broad-wing even more rarely, but the red-shoulder, which most closely resembles the rough-leg in form when wings and tail are spread, apparently not all. Indeed, the rough-leg is so adept at stationary "flight" it can, if conditions are right, hang in the air almost as well as the white-tailed kite of the deep south; and that bird's ability has drawn exclamations of wonder from me. I saw one rough-leg remain so suspended while it endured the several attacks of one hundred or so starlings, a massed flock moving as one bird. But it can also move quite speedily. One dusk I was forced to travel eighty kilometres per hour to keep abreast of one flying parallel to my road.

The rough-leg is a gregarious species, one family party attracting another until quite a loose flock will have gathered about some area on the tundra. If it appears that the hunting will prove poor, they may migrate *en masse* and although such southward flights are not made in the same manner as that of the broad-wing, they have supplied thousands of targets to trigger-happy outdoorsmen in the past. Even now, "varmint" shooters take a heavy and illegal toll by potting birds as they perch on poles and posts, favored resting spots, although tree and ground roosts are used indiscriminately.

While wintering with us in the settled parts of Canada and the United States, the rough-leg is virtually silent, but in summer will stupidly advise all comers of the presence of its nest, being as voluble as the red-tail on such occasions. From various reports, its cry at such times sounds like the *me-aow* of an angry young kitten, while its Eskimo name translates into "squalling hawk."

Another good name for it would be "window-box hawk." In the more northern,

LIGHT PHASE

DARK PHASE

treeless regions, it uses cliff ledges for nesting, laying on a scanty foundation which is usually higher at the front. This may be contrived engineering to keep the eggs from rolling off, but is more probably because rough-legs are poor housekeepers, some of the nest material consisting of bones and other refuse liberally sprinkled with excrement, all of it deposited or shoved to the outer edge. The rich nutrients in the accumulation foster considerable plant growth, so that any green spot on a cliff ledge will be, in all probability, the garden of a pair of rough-legged buzzards.

Despite all the written accounts, it does not confine its diet to mice which it swallows headfirst with ease. We were driving through farmland one winter day when three rough-legs were spotted perched on consecutive fence posts in from the highway. Wondering about the concentration, we stopped, to find the attraction a European hare calmly sitting hard against the strands of wire. From time to time one of the birds would leave its perch and attempt to capture the mammal. But none of the three had sufficient acumen to make a frontal approach. All flew parallel to the fence, an act that forced them to stay at least a wing's length from it. The hare imperturbably looked up from under the extended wing, smirking like a toned-down Bugs Bunny.

A taste for southern lagomorphs is not exceptional, apparently, as James F. Traynor, writing in *The Conservationist* of November-December, 1977, found rough-legs taking rabbits in his Albany, New York area. He also tells of a party of five engaging in a rough-house aerial play much as do ravens. I may have seen something similar but the birds were too far away for positive identification.

Golden Eagle (*Aquila chrysaëtos*)

Summers from the Arctic shores of Alaska and Canada south down the cordillera into Mexico and along the west side of the Great Plains in United States; also in the Laurentian Shield in Canada and the Appalachian Mountains in United States. In the eastern hemisphere, south to the east-west cordillera but absent from western lowlands. In the western hemisphere may winter in any wilderness section of the whole of United States and Canada.

The immaculate sky was sullied only by a distant speck that, growing larger with incredible speed, crossed the highway some distance from us, disappeared behind a rise, reappeared shrugging off a pair of inimical crows and then turned, to sail high above the surface of Kamloops Lake, in British Columbia. Standing on an eminence, of which that province has quite a few, we left off contemplating a paradoxical panorama of water, near-desert and land forever tilting, and watched the majestic approach of a bird quite contemptuous of protocol. The imperator reversed roles and sailed regally by us, two commoners taking the salute on the reviewing stand. The "ring-tail," an immature golden eagle from one to three years old, passed us at eye level, no more than two hundred metres away, thrilling us more than any "first" entered in our journals.

In North America, the golden eagle is, primarily, a western bird, ruling over a wild kingdom of unscalable mountains and unworkable foothills. It avoids the flat prairies but appears again in the east wherever the country is quasi-mountainous and indubitably wild. In the west, the nature of the terrain and the bird's tolerance for others of its kind mean that a pair is content with a territory of one-tenth the extent of its requirements in the east. There it pre-empts a forested area large enough so that the scattered patches of open land it contains will total the unforested area used by a pair of birds in the west.

To see a golden eagle in the east, one must clamber the rocky, inhospitable fastness of Ungava and Labrador; or spend a lifetime scouring eastern skies in fond expectancy of sighting a migrating or wintering bird. For the golden eagle is tolerant of cold, wintering where other diurnal birds of prey could not subsist. About one hundred years ago several specimens were taken in the Parry Sound District of Ontario in the months of November through March, no balmy period in that area. The scarcity of the bird suggests such records will never be equalled. However, most of the eastern breeders do move south, adding to the zest of hawkwatchers at Hawk Mountain, Pennsylvania, and at Hawk Cliff and Point Pelee, Ontario and other points of vantage.

The unpredictability of its movements has been noted in my personal journals. One August day, paddling to a point on our lake in Muskoka, Ontario, I was startled by the appearance of an eagle. At first, I took it for a plane which frequently approached the lake from that direction, even though the plane was white and the bird was dark! The eagle soared a short distance out over the lake, then turned, to sail back from whence it came, its wings seeming like two ironing boards, while a flash of tawny reflected from its head.

Everywhere, the golden eagle has suffered the fate of all massive birds and mammals. Birds have been shot for no other reason than to add to the ego of the gun-wielder, who is then proudly photographed holding the bird in such a way as to display its wingspread of two metres. It has been shot, poisoned and trapped, because it is thought to have an exorbitant taste for the young of livestock. Undeniably, the golden eagle is a formidable antagonist, for birds wintering in the north have attacked wolves, but more often such assaults are successful only through the cooperative efforts of two birds, just as the African crowned hawk eagles trap monkeys. One of those birds will wait on a perch while the other flies over a troup, distracting their attention until a monkey exposes itself and enables the other bird to seize him. Such cooperation may not be necessary when the very young of mountain sheep and goats, deer and domestic livestock are attacked and killed. But when such reports are studied, it is evident that the longer the kid, calf, lamb or fawn has survived, the less likely it is to be set upon; and, as is common with other predators, both feathered and furred, desperation is the catalyst of the attack. Stealing, it must be remembered, is not unknown among very hungry humans. In both cases, improved wardenship is the best deterrent.

The breeding range of the golden eagle coincides with the presence of some form of ground squirrel, marmot and/or hare, proliferation of which is checked by the birds, a fact that has not penetrated the minds of many western ranchers. The golden eagle finds it difficult, if not impossible, to carry off animals larger than a woodchuck. It has been demonstrated that eight pounds is the maximum it can carry, which rules out stories that it has carted off young children. In the unrecorded history of man there may have

ADULT

IMMATURE

been times when an infant, left on the ground while its mother gathered firewood or berries, was attacked by an eagle. Such accounts would have been retold with colorful embellishments, around many a campfire until the printing press took over and accepted them factually, but that is just my unsubstantiated theory.

In spite of being gunned down from planes, in spite of a reproductive rate that sees a pair raise only a fraction more than one bird annually, the golden eagle does not, as yet, seem to be an endangered species. If it is, it is blithely unaware of it, still indulging in death-defying dives. This exhibition of its mastery over mere atmosphere is given not only on nuptial occasions or when a pair reaffirm their vows, but also through the year, an emotive release indicative of a zest for living. There was no other reason for an adult to make two such dives over Mississauga, Ontario, in September, 1971, bringing me and my car to an abrupt halt.

American Kestrel (*Falco sparverius*)

Summers from near the tree limit in Alaska and Canada south through most of Central America and the West Indies to the tip of South America. Absent from the Amazon forest. In winter, withdraws toward the Equator, in the Northern Hemisphere remaining north as far as southern British Columbia and Ontario and the states as far north as the Great Lakes.

So ingrained are habits that, despite the change in the common name of this little falcon, effected in 1973 by the American Ornithologists Union, my pocket notebook still contains the cryptic notation, "Sp. H." This is short-longhand for "Sparrow Hawk," and occurs with considerable frequency, for this falcon, which long labored under one of the major faults of nomenclature perpetrated by man, ranks with the red-tail as the hawk most frequently seen. And, it might be added, heard.

According to Winsor Marrett Tyler, writing in Bent, the early North American colonists saw in this bird a reproduction of the European sparrow-hawk, a misconception scarcely credible. The similarity of the two birds begins and ends in size, once one dispenses with the incontestable fact that both are clothed in feathers. The mistake in nomenclature seems even more incredible when we consider that both our sharp-shinned and Cooper's hawks bear a far greater resemblance to the European sparrow-hawk, which is understandable as all three are accipiters. And it becomes even more unbelievable because our kestrel scarcely differs from the Old World kestrel in habits, and is unlike that bird largely in being blue of wing and rusty of tail, reversing the colors of the bird so well known throughout Europe, Asia and Africa.

Our brightly-hued falcon, whose extravagant colors are at variance with the more somber patterns of most North American hawks, is the roadside hawk par eminence. It assumes that telephone and other utility wires were strung for its use exclusively. (I assume that it avoids electrocution because it never has one foot on the ground at the same time). The favored wires are those adjacent to fields and open country. But the little falcon persistently pops up in the most surprising places. One summer day a kestrel materialized over a small forest-fringed lake in pursuit of a goshawk. The only piece of open land I knew to be in that area was four hundred metres distant, a narrow road, sometimes paralleled by a hydro right-of-way, both slicing through bush as dense as that surrounding the lake.

There is nothing self-effacing about the kestrel. In addition to wearing colorful feathers, it is the noisiest of our hawks. Its volubility knows neither season nor locality. A disyllabic and oft-repeated *killy-killy-killy* is the usual transcription, but some authors hear the call as a *kee-kee-kee.* The reception doubtless depends on the ear of the listener. For instance, my wife insists the bird whistles, throwing me into such confusion that I will turn from one giving its staccato cry and ask her, in puzzlement, "What did you say is whistling?"

The kestrel can leave its lookout on a wire or stub, pick up a luckless victim from a grassy field and be back on its perch in a trice. Sometimes, though, the mouse, sparrow, grasshopper or whatever will change position, whereupon the kestrel will literally stand still in the air, awaiting a more favorable opportunity for its lethal pounce. It does not hang motionless, like a kite, but hovers on rapidly beating wings, its body on about a forty-five degree angle. I have lined up such a bird against a pole or wire and have seen no change of position for as much as a minute. Then it will either complete its drop or

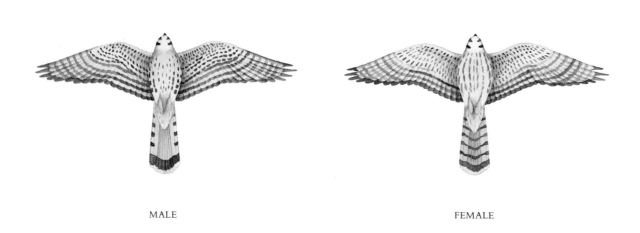

MALE   FEMALE

return to a perch and its ceaseless vigil, characteristically pumping its tail on alighting. "Windhover," an apt appellation, is a name commonly given to the British kestrel and sometimes to ours.

Another well-deserved name is "grasshopper hawk," these insects forming the bulk of its food in proper season. At other times, it is the scourge of the meadow vole, the rodent that sustains most of the kestrels that winter in snow-covered countrysides. Not a few fall from grace and pick up the odd tree sparrow or other small bird of the winter's fields. A few, too, will become temporary urbanites and will live on the house sparrows, starlings, house mice and Norway rats infesting certain communities. Still fewer will pick up an occasional meal at a garden feeding station. I have been spared the sight of the actual attack but presume the three or four I have seen speeding away from my feeders were successful.

From the foregoing, it may be correctly inferred that the kestrel will suffer the presence of humans. It will do even more, readily nesting in boxes of suitable dimensions, as this is our only hawk, other than an occasional merlin, that nests in cavities. The combination of lookout-wire and old woodpecker nest in a wood pole is irrestible to the kestrel.

Brown and Amadon state it is antisocial except prior to nesting, when three or four will coexist amicably. This is at variance with my observations during the hawk movements of September, when as many as four have been seen in the same dead elm, six about the same field and ten in a narrow radius. In mid-November, the day before completing this essay, I saw two, side by side on the same wire. Because of the dates, none of these groups could have been family parties. In late August, well before the beginning of the hawk migration, I have seen four fly over the same large field and considered them united by family ties. When two engaged in mock combat, I concluded the birds were siblings participating in post-graduate nest exercises.

The American kestrel is a despotic bird, quick to attack other feathered predators for no reason other than it resents their presence. But one harsh winter day I saw a kestrel harass one of a pair of crows, forcing it to drop a mouse. It also vents displeasure on small birds, whose equanimity seems unruffled until the bird-eating season arrives. Then they will scatter in alarm. Still, all birds will ignore the rules they, themselves, have established, for I once saw a kestrel permit a least flycatcher to share the same branch while sending all other small birds haunting the same field into frenzied flight.

Merlin (*Falco columbarius*)

Summers from just beyond the tree limit in North America, Europe and Asia south to or just below the Canadian border (but not south-western Ontario) and the Eurasian cordillera; also down the western ranges into northern California. Winters south to or just beyond the Equator on both continents.

From the time of Audubon and Wilson until just a few years ago, this small falcon, the bird allotted to the ladies during the turbulent days when falconry served as a tranquilizer, was called "pigeon hawk" in North America. Thus, this continent had its duck hawk, sparrow hawk and pigeon hawk, the inference being that each one was named for its food preference. This was true only in the case of the duck hawk, now known universally as the peregrine falcon. The sparrow hawk, or American kestrel, rarely touches birds of any kind, although certain individuals living close to an urban life may subsist to a large degree on house sparrows in winter. And to avoid the tussle that would ensue, the merlin rarely takes pigeons, preferring birds somewhat smaller. Food preferences, then, were not the origin of its former name. But its appearance and action in flight are remarkably pigeon–like, hence its still popular cognomen. Fortunately, all our falcons have rid themselves of the word "hawk," a name that should be restricted to the accipiters. The conversion of our buteos to "buzzards" will also be a happy event.

The merlin is a hawk of the open, the prairie grassland, the beaches and cultivated fields. Over such country it hunts pipits, horned larks, longspurs and the smaller sandpipers. It is a pursuer rather than a stooper, following a flock until, with its sharp, cutting wing-stroke driving it at terrific speed, it will be upon and through the assembled birds before they have an inkling of the falcon's presence. On emergence it will be clutching its next meal and has been seen to come out with two, one in each foot.

If the flock scatters in alarm, even before the attack proper, the falcon will set out after some individual with such tenacity of purpose that one can but admire its perseverance. It cannot, of course, cope with a bird adept at dodging and soon leaves off chasing quarry capable of corkscrew flight.

The merlin is a feathered bundle of inexhaustible energy, suggesting, in its hunting chase, tremendous reserves. When not hungry, it must use up nervous energy by harassing game it customarily pursues or birds so much larger than itself it could not hope to subdue them. Crows, ravens and other hawks are harried without provocation.

The same energetic excitement pervades when humans enter the general vicinity of its home. Not content with concealing its nest in a tree cavity, a depression on the ground under a tree, or in the abandoned nest of a crow, jay or magpie, it must meet the intruder when still some distance away, the excitement in its shrill cries ample evidence of the reason for its concern.

While the merlin hunts over treeless regions, it does make use of large woody growth for nesting, but the nest tree, if one is used at all, even for concealing a ground nest, will be at the edge of a forest or within a small grove surrounded by open country.

In fact, the merlin has such little use for trees that it rarely perches on one, preferring instead a rock, stump or even the ground. It was during a methodical sweep of a lake, seeking waterfowl, that I picked up one in my telescope not so long ago. The bird, atop a partially submerged stump, was tearing into the flesh of some unidentified victim, and

ADULT   IMMATURE

as I watched, I realized that I had been seeing more merlins of late. A little research into my records would have delighted a statistician. I have seen exactly twice as many merlins in the past twenty years as I had in the same period preceding. But statistics do not say why, and that is what I'd like to know.

Gyrfalcon (*Falco rusticolus*)

Found north of the tree-line on both continents. Sporadically winters farther south, barely penetrating the northern tier of states or crossing the Eurasian cordillera.

Were it not for the health problems of the peregrine falcon, the gyr would be the rarest hawk of regular occurrence in the settled parts of eastern North America. It is a bird of the Arctic, both high and low, representing the hawks there as the snowy owl does the nocturnal raptors. The falcon's principal prey are the willow and rock ptarmigan, closely followed by the snow bunting, and then the Arctic and varying hares. The two ptarmigan are partially or irregularly migratory and are thus pursued by the falcon as the grouse change location according to the season. All five food items experience irregularity in population numbers, declining due to adverse conditions or to partially unexplained cyclic crashes. Under mitigating circumstances brought on by food shortages, the gyrfalcon will then move south, reaching but rarely crossing the Great Lakes. This is the time when food preferences are necessarily shelved for anything in feathers. However, it still prefers treeless or sparsely grown areas and finds places like long, wind-swept beaches particularly attractive.

Unpredictable as may be its appearance in the south, one staged a faithful show at Toronto in early 1978. The curtain rose late in the afternoon with an exhibition of a duck's capture from the proliferation of waterfowl on the harbor, the matinee concluding with supper on the roof of a warehouse.

The etymology of its name is very devious, according to Gruson. It has no relation to gyro (we meet the circle again but quickly disassociate ourselves from geometry!) but is instead related to greedy. Rather than to spell the prefix "gyr," or the older "heiro," the simpler "ger" would be preferred, thus eliminating numerous corrections in pronunciation. Indeed, we might go farther and call it "partridge hawk," a name immediately recognizable to all northern peoples and to whom gyr (that is, ger) falcon is a foreign expression.

The gyrfalcon was the one preferred by kings when both chivalry and falconry were in favor. Since most birds were captured in eastern Greenland, the difficulty in obtaining them must have been immense. Yet, the authors of 700 years ago knew as much of the bird's life history as we do now!

This falcon ordinarily cruises at a slower rate of speed than does the peregrine, but during its attack, which usually is a pursuit rather than a stoop from above, will reach speeds unattained by anything else in feathers. The force of its blow can be heard as a sharp *crack*, while the breast-bone of its victim is almost invariably broken. Its short, rapid, but powerful wing-beats are interspersed with short sails.

A description of its nest is quickly dispensed with for two reasons. Only intrepid northern explorers or inhabitants will see it; and, anyway, it builds none, a characteristic of the falcons. What appears to be a nest is an accumulation of excrement and inedible bones. In the treeless regions it utilizes a rocky ledge complete with overhanging snow-shed, although it is not averse to using a fabrication abandoned by or pre-empted from ravens or rough-legged hawks. A rock face well marked by excreta and a ledge

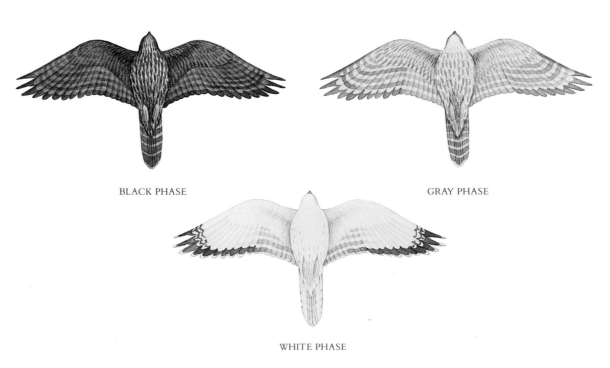

BLACK PHASE

GRAY PHASE

WHITE PHASE

94

decorated by a green window-box is well worth investigation, if travel in the land of the Aurora Borealis is your inclination.

And there, too, is the only place you will hear its staccato, rasping *keks*.

Peregrine Falcon (*Falco peregrinus*)

Summers from the Arctic regions of both hemispheres south into Mexico and to the Eurasian cordillera; also the tip of South America and all except the dry portions of Africa, the Middle East, Asia and Australia. In North America, winters chiefly south of Canada to northern South America and the West Indies.

Doctors Brown and Amadon endorsed the views of the great majority of ornithologists, both professional and amateur, when, in their revision of the order *Falconiformes*, they placed the peregrine falcon at the pinnacle, signifying it has ascended higher in the ladder of evolution than any other diurnal raptor.

The peregrine truly rules the air, outspeeding even swifts and swallows, those proponents of rapid flight. When Tennyson, poeticizing the golden eagle, penned, "And like a thunderbolt it falls" it was obvious he had never seen the stoop of a peregrine. Bent records an incident where the aviator of a small plane, diving playfully on a flock of ducks, reached a speed of 280 kilometres per hour – and was passed by a peregrine intent on a meal!

In early October some years ago, I was watching the constant movement of bird migrants gathered at Point Pelee's extensive marsh, when no less than three peregrines gave an exhibition of flight equalling that of any air show. An osprey, flapping across the marsh, wary eye on two bald eagles circling on high, suddenly found itself under attack from another quarter, as one of the falcons opted for a game of tag. Several times the big fish hawk was struck, although perhaps "tapped" would be a better word, as the falcon had play, not food, in mind. The osprey was forced into a somewhat wavering flight nevertheless. Both peregrine and merlin believe that all work and no play makes for a dull ploy.

Their display of speed on that occasion was at variance to the flight of the first peregrine I ever saw, a performance emphasizing that birds are forever stepping out of character. During the programmed field trip of a naturalists' convention held near Toronto in the early thirties, a large hawk flapped across a field, perched momentarily on a tree, then flapped on its way, with all the mannerisms of a large buteo. Since the dash of a falcon was nowhere in attendance, all except the two leaders of the party were wavering between naming the bird a red-tail or red-shoulder. Indecision was erased by the shout from one of the two leaders: "A duck hawk!" Immediate confirmation came from the other conductor, equally expert, who had also caught the Fu Manchu mustache, a feature overlooked by the rest of us.

In early May of 1971, another duck hawk (long the name of the North American bird) seen flying under restraint, crossed a body of water, turned right with some hesitation, then flew directly over my head as if it had found some discrepancy in its filed flight plan. This bird has always puzzled me because peregrines were considered extirpated from the east by that time. In all probability, it was one of the Arctic subspecies en route to its far northern home.

The peregrine requires its exceptional speed awing in order to overtake or dive

ADULT   IMMATURE

upon its prey of birds, for it rarely eats anything else. Small birds are caught in the air. Larger ones are simply knocked out of it. The latter are struck and raked by the hind claws just as the hawk begins to climb after its stoop. The falcon approaches its quarry from above, drops to slightly below it, then passes over it on its ascent, so that, after the blow, it may turn to follow it, catching its victim well above the ground. In event of a miss, it will continue on a rising plane so that it may repeat its game plan.

Because of its predilection for feathered life, the best places to watch for peregrines are where birds pass during migration or congregate in summer. Point Pelee, as mentioned previously, and similar areas about the Great Lakes, were ideal spots before the species was extirpated as a breeding bird from all of eastern North America south of Ungava. Those breeding farther north may be seen to advantage when they pass along the Atlantic coast in the wake of shorebirds in the fall. A few still follow the inland routes and regularly thrill the watchers manning popular hawk-viewing points.

In its hey-day, the juxtaposition of a cliff ledge (its preferred nest-site) and plentiful bird life, enhanced the possibility of seeing one in summer. Wilderness was not a prerequisite, however, as the species, quite content with a diet of street pigeons, starlings and house sparrows, found the window ledges of modern skyscrapers as acceptable as any cliff overlooking a marsh. Such incongruous sites were used in Boston, Chicago, New York, Philadelphia, Harrisburg (Pennsylvania) and Montreal, where a nest on the Sun Life building was used for seventeen consecutive years.

The factors relating to its diminishing numbers are related elsewhere. Geographically, the decline was not uniform and certainly not as devasting in some regions as it was in northeastern North America, where the subspecies *anatum*, the so-called eastern peregrine falcon, has been extirpated. Fortunately, the subspecies still exists, although precariously, to the west and northwest of the area covered herein.

Where some species have quickly rebounded from catastrophic losses (the eastern bluebird did so twice), the peregrine has been unable to overcome the high mortality of its young birds, two-thirds of which usually do not survive their first year. Then, as three years elapse before the survivors are in a breeding condition, the number of new birds capable of procreating do not equal those lost to disease, shooting and old age. Contributing to the continued decline are not only the loss of habitat but, in the opinion of Gerald McKeating, a biologist with the Ministry of Natural Resources in Ottawa, their sensitivity to habitat changes, as their requirements seem highly specialized.

In the English-speaking world and in Europe, the peregrine was the *ne plus ultra* among falconers. And while this sport is no longer in vogue (there is, however, a current re-awakening), its popularity is high enough that young peregrines are still sought, and obtained, by unscrupulous means. Fortunately, only a very few of present-day falconers perpetrate nest depredations; nor do they engage in egg-napping, still a threat to falcons and other birds in Britain. But, as in the case of the whooping crane, where the value of every bird is incalculable, the violation of any peregrine's nest is a serious matter and should not be countenanced.

The Owls

The Owls

There are 132, 133 or 134 distinct kinds of owls in the world depending on the authority to which you have pledged allegiance. Like the diurnal raptors, they are missing from some oceanic islands and from the continent of Antarctica. One species, the great horned owl, occurs in various subspecies throughout the western hemisphere, from the Straits of Magellan to within the Arctic Circle, where it is replaced from there to possibly the North Pole by the entirely different snowy owl. A handful of species is circumpolar or holarctic, the Eurasian form or forms differing from the North American by, at times, obscure characters. A few North American species have Eurasian analogues, our great horned owl being replaced by the eagle owl, our screech by the scops and our barred and spotted owls by the tawny.

The order to which the owls are assigned is called *Strigiformes*, a quite distinctive one with no known affinities except, possibly, the goatsuckers. Relationship to the hawks is dim and very ancient. Eleven of North America's eighteen kinds of owls have been included herein, the omissions being, as in the case of the hawks, species with which artist and author have little familiarity. The limitation of space is another factor in both cases.

Throughout the world, the entire order of owls is, in general, quite sedentary. All members are equipped, physically, to survive intense cold, the one factor influencing any seasonal movement being the supply of food, which is, in some respect, related to temperature. Thus, if the food supply falls below the level required by the number of owls of one species living within a region, some will have to move elsewhere or starve. Such movements are periodic (every four, five or six years or more) and depend, naturally, on the type of food they usually seek.

Likewise, young owls of the year move, sometimes considerable distances from their birthplace, forced from the place of their nativity because of lack of room. Only when one or both parents have died will the young owl be inclined to take over the old homestead, provided, of course, it can wrest it from its siblings.

There are a few kinds of owls, however, that migrate habitually. The highly insectivorous scops owl is obliged to vacate its summer home in the southern parts of Europe and journey to Africa. Some oriental hawk owls (not the same as the bird of that name of the northern hemisphere) move north toward the equator to spend their winter months of June, July and August. The two eared owls have migratory tendencies which may be, in part, seasonal, in part the necessity of concentration in some region affording easy prey in the form of superabundant voles. Still, no explanation can be advanced for the flight of one long-eared owl from California to Ontario.

Because owls are so nocturnal, they have been popularly endowed with the ability to see in absolute darkness and, conversely, they are believed to be unable to see in daylight. Both suppositions are completely erroneous. Like humans, any owl moving from dark to brilliant surroundings will be dazzled and will require an appreciable length of time to adjust to the change. Humans will also be aware that when even the slightest bit of light is admitted into a darkened room, their eyes will receive, at the least, a shadowy substance of their surroundings.

The following is an attempt to explain the amazing eyesight of owls in a language shorn of the terminology of an ophthalmologist, for the complexity of the whole arrangement is too great to detail here.

The eyes of owls collect and concentrate more light than the eyes of a diurnal species. It is a large eye (that of the larger owls is as large as a human's), with a relatively large "window," the system of cornea and lens. The retina is relatively closer to the lens than in a man's eye, retaining a brighter image. To protect their sensitive retina, which is analogous to the sensitized plate of camera film, the iris of owls contracts in bright light, expanding when more light has to be admitted. Like nocturnal mammals, owls probably have a second reflecting structure, the tapetum, which will pick up light not absorbed and pass it on to the sensitive cells which, in turn, connect with the optic nerve. It is the tapetum that causes the eyes of night prowlers, such as cats, to shine in the dark.

The retina is composed of light-sensitive cells in the form of rods and cones. The rods, the more sensitive of the two, function when the light is too weak to stimulate the cones, which are responsible for sharp images and color. Obviously, a day bird or mammal will have more cones than rods. They will also be able to "read" more detail. When the retina is predominately of rod formation, the animal will be nocturnal, normally unable to see the "fine" print. Owls confuse scientists because they are able to see well not only at night, but better and in more detail than man can by day!

Owls are unable to move the eye within its socket, replacing the normal eye movement with a rapid swivelling of the head, turning it, if necessary, up to 270 degrees. In addition, the owl's flat face, with the eyes directed forward, gives it monocular vision, like man's, and unlike the robin's, which, with eyes on the sides of its head, sees two images at one time.

While the eyesight of an owl may be fantastic and its flight uncanny, its most singular feature is its phenomenal hearing. Its ears are not the tufts of feathers to be found on the heads of some species, but are like those of other birds, openings situated on the sides of the head and covered with soft, loose feathers. In owls, however, the auricular opening is much larger than that of any other bird. In some essentially nocturnal species it stretches from near the top of the cranium to the lower jaw, a lunar-shaped opening almost girdling the skull. Flaps, functioning like the hand of a person cupping one ear, fringe the opening, the front one being quite mobile and possibly serving to improve the reception of sounds originating in the rear.

The flat face of an owl is the result of its facial disc, that somewhat circular fringe or ruff of feathers encircling the face. These feathers can be raised or depressed as the owl samples each sound wave, much as does a dog or cat with its ears, turning them to better funnel sounds into the ear drum.

Those humans who have a great appreciation of symmetrical form, will consign owls to a low place on the scale of design. In some species, one ear opening may be larger than the other; in another species, one may be higher than the other; while in a third, one will be upside down! This difference in symmetry, added to the large size of the head, results in an appreciable time lag in the reception between the two ears and permits the bird to zero in on the slight sound of a mouse rustling amidst leaves. The ear-flaps as well are not always symmetrical, improving hearing still more. The more nocturnal the species, the better developed is its facial disc and the more asymmetrical its ear flaps and openings. The high-pitched squeak of a mouse may have no impact on the tympanum of a human, but will turn an owl's thoughts to the dinner hour. At the same time, the owl may only "feel" the beat of a tuba or contra bass, unable to tell if the right note was struck.

Like a few other kinds of birds, such as flycatchers, owls have bristles at the base of the bill which suggest some sense of touch. Such "whiskers," common in nocturnal and subterranean mammals, which use them in feeling their way in the dark, may be used by the owl for the same purpose. In some species they may have a double function, to feel and to trap insects in the same way that flycatchers, nighthawks and whip-poor-wills catch their food. The screech-scops owl complex catch air-borne insects with the bill rather than with the feet.

The most serious study of owls has contributed nothing to support the ages-old theory that they possess wisdom. The closest approach to sapience has been found in a barred owl that frequented Toronto's Central YMCA, even to entering a room for shelter. Appropriately, it earned the sobriquet, the "Y's Owl."

Owls have four toes, the usual number among birds, but arrange them in zygodactyl fashion, two toes being directed forward, two backward, like old-fashioned ice-tongs. Woodpeckers, toucans, cuckoos and parrots have the same arrangement, one of the reasons owls are thought to be related, albeit distantly, to the last two groups. Except for a few species that use the bill to catch insects, owls, like hawks, use the foot to seize prey and, to better adjust to its squirming and the outer toe of owls is reversible, a feature found in toucans and the osprey. The African and Asian fishing owls have spicules on the undersides of the toes, as does the osprey, to assist in holding their slippery prey. The larger the victim, the bigger and stronger the feet. The Akun eagle owl of Africa, which eats almost nothing but insects, has weak feet and bill, yet is the same size and occupies much the same range as Fraser's eagle owl, a mammal eater with much stronger bill and talons.

Other than a few exceptions, such as those mentioned, there is a marked lack of diversity in the feet of owls, suggesting that, unlike the diurnal raptors, there is little variety in their prey and the mode of attack. They hunt usually from perches and at quite close quarters.

There are several freebooters among birds. The bald eagle frequently pirates the osprey; the skua and jaegers plunder the gulls; and the gulls themselves are Jolly Roger characters. Perhaps because owls' nocturnal life makes them more difficult to observe, piracy seems to have been noted in only one instance. A pearl-spotted owlet of Africa skulked about the nest of a wood hoopoe, awaiting its return with food. The owl's furious attack would bowl the hoopoe over, easily dislodging the food it was carrying.

Owls have a tendency to near-cannibalism, with any owl capturing and eating a species smaller than itself. There is evidence that the burrowing owl of the North American prairies occasionally indulges in true cannibalism, the eating of its own species.

As owls tend to bolt their prey entire, the bill sees little use as a butchering instrument. Larger owls use it to decapitate small prey and to render large items, while possibly all will use it to end the struggles of a victim insensitive to the talons piercing its innards. As a threat against a formidable antagonist, such as a human, an owl overlooks such dangerous weapons as talons and beak and instead will fluff out its feathers and rattle its mandibles menacingly. Bill clicking figures in other displays as well.

The success of owls in the role of nocturnal predators is due to their phenomenal hearing and their silent progress through the air. The wing-loading, the relationship between wing area and body weight, is low for owls. In the ring-necked pheasant, a bird about the same bulk as a great horned owl, the ratio is high, forcing it to rapid, energetic wing-beats to gain progress. The owl's equal weight is supported by a much greater wing expanse, meaning an immediate reduction in flight noise. In addition, the flight feathers of the owl have a surface suggesting a thick pile, with soft fringes on their leading edges. Air can slip through without whistling, while the whole wing is designed to permit the passage of air without friction. The more nocturnal the owl, the more strongly developed are the silencers. Owlets and pygmy owls, the fishing owls and the North American hawk owl are more diurnal species and, with less need for silent flight, can be heard while in the air, although they still produce far less noise than does a pheasant.

The owl's soundless flight is doubly beneficial. Its quarry has no warning of impending disaster nor does the owl have the sound of its own movements drown out those of its prey. Like hawks with broad wings, owls have some primaries emarginate, which slotting reduces air turbulence at the wing tips and minimizes stalling.

Members of the genus *Asio* have relatively long wings to assist in their migratory habits, ill-defined though they may be.

The two groups of raptorial birds differ widely in threat posture. Where hawks stand up boldly, opening the wings as if preparing for an embrace, owls will lower the head, spreading the wings so that the upper surface is presented. The action of the hawk is one of defiance. While it is largely bluff, it does suggest that an attack is imminent. The owl's action leaves you guessing but you sense that homicide seems seriously contemplated, perhaps initiated with a charge reminiscent of an infuriated bull. The barred owl makes puzzling use of the wing, raising one to shield its face while keeping the other close to its body. The person to have first seen this must have been strongly imaginative, as there has been passed down through literature the word that the owl greatly resembles a mammal at such time. Manipulate the wing of a skin as you will, it is unlikely you will get the same impression.

In 1896, Abbot H. Thayer established the principle of counter shading, his thesis being that an animal is darkest where it receives the most light, palest where it receives the least. The many shorebirds are the best examples among birds. Note that this group stands, moves and flies with the body quite horizontal, far different to the almost vertical pose of owls. They, because of their upright posture, have both front and back patterned with streaks, bars and blotches, the feathers being marked with shades of brown, buff, sepia and cream. True black and true white are rarely present except in one species, while rufous and rusty are the most vivid colors to be found within the order. Their plumage imitates the branches, twigs and foliage, streaked and dappled with heavily filtered light, but colorless in the dim surroundings of the forest. It is an excellent example of Thayer's second law, that the pattern of markings must be a picture of the background against which the bird is seen by its prey or enemies. Counter shading, if any, is exhibited only on the lower part of the belly, the breast then being barred and streaked, but in a pattern different to that of the back.

Some owls are marked so as to duplicate the bark of trees against which they normally huddle. In addition, many species increase the already effective concealment pattern by drawing in the feathers to elongate the body and, with eyes narrowed to slits, will seem to be a broken stub. Burrowing, short-eared and African marsh owls exhibit some degree of counter shading, with underparts paler than the back. They will not sit as closely as quail but do place some reliance on their resemblance to the ground on which they habitually nest. The snowy owl blends well with the snow. In the Arctic spring, the female, black-flecked where the male is an almost immaculate white, merges into the patchwork of snow and newly exposed ridges of the tundra and is therefore difficult to detect when incubating.

These various subterfuges are more frequently penetrated by small birds than by humans. Chickadees and blue jays are adept at spotting such owls, which infintely prefer to be ignored than to be the target of titmouse and garruline vituperatives. If the abuse becomes too excessive, the owl will seek other quarters, perhaps moving more than once, in order to resume its slumbers. Crows delight in zeroing in on great horned owls, which endears them to birders anxious to tick the name of the great horned on their annual bird list. Anyone interested in seeing an owl of any kind should follow up such crowds of jabbering birds.

Retaliation does occur. Ernest Thompson Seton's famed crow, Silverspot, lost its life to its archenemy, while down in the Argentine, the ferruginous owl is credited with hypnotizing small birds, commanding them to approach still closer until, with a flashing talon, one tormentor disappears from the list.

In the final stages of preparing this book the fact that the southern states lack the same kind of cover (dense evergreens, for example) that exists in the north was drawn to my attention. Parts of both Florida and Texas are subtropical, yet far removed from the tropical rain-forests where the most colorful birds can disappear with the flick of a wing. And tall as is the stately royal palm, it cannot hope to conceal a hawk or owl as well as a leafy sugar maple. The latter trees were in the back of my mind while I was being led to a grove of "big trees" in Texas. Suddenly I found myself in a grove of trees whose size and shape were reminiscent of the apple tree in my garden, the most apparent difference being the extreme girth of the trunk.

Old the trees may have been, but shelters for owls they were not. In fact, in retrospect, I don't know where in that neighborhood an owl could have sought refuge. Which may be why, a short time later, my wife spotted a great horned owl perched on a thick, lower limb of a live oak, perhaps six feet from the trunk. The bird both confused and amused me. I was confused because the horned owl of my northern experience hid from me in the thick confines of a conifer; and I was tickled because it seemed to be saying, "What's the use? Might as well perch here as in that skimpy thicket over there." Owl-finding must be a very simple matter in the deep south.

Many birds have white outer tail-feathers or white patches in the wings or on the rump. These are thought to be markings to confuse a predator, the flashes disappearing as soons as the bird comes to rest in a thicket or on the ground. They are also thought to be signals to others of the same kind, serving to guide a flock. In either case, such markings would be of little value to owls, not only because they are the pursuers rather than the pursued, but because flashes of white could not be seen in their normally gloomy surroundings. Understandably, owl communication is vocal rather than visual. The goatsuckers, which bear some relationship to owls, are also cryptically colored and, like them, active at night. But theirs is a constant activity where, in their flight, banner marks or recognition signals are displayed in wings, tail or throat, alone or in combination. The more passive owl advertises itself visually, by silhouette. Forty-four per cent of the world's owls have ear-tufts which, in conjunction with size, present shapes recognizable not only to owls but to human owl-watchers.

American pygmy owls have markings on the back of the head greatly resembling a second set of eyes. These have a startling effect on humans but their purpose in the wild is obscure. What is more interesting is the coincidence that the pygmy owl and the American kestrel have four points in common: Small size, rear eye-spots, addiction to nesting in cavities and the habit of tail-flicking. It may be that a nest intruder is repelled by the sight of large eyes no matter which way the nesting bird is facing. This explanation could suffice for the kestrel, as the male does some incubating, but not for the owl, as the male does none and therefore has no need for such spots.

The ferruginous owl of southwestern North America, South and Central America, has a white spot below and on each side of the bill. According to Argentinian natives, these are eyebrows, the dark spots below them a second set of eyes, giving the owl super vision. "Four-eyes" was a term of ridicule bestowed on scholars obliged to wear glasses during the early years of schooling. Is the ferruginous owl subjected to similar abuse by its relatives?

Dichromatism, a state in which a species has two color phases, is common in two genera of owls: *Otus*, the screech-scops owl complex and *Glaucidium*, the owlet-pygmy owl group. It seems confined, in the latter, to Indian and Oriental owlets and to certain Caribbean and Central and South American species, including North America's ferruginous owl. It is far more common and wide-spread in *Otus*, with our well-known screech owl and, to a lesser extent, the European scops owl, offering the best examples. The birds may be predominately gray or a shade of reddish brown, apparently ungoverned by law, with both phases found in the same brood regardless of the color of the parents. One phase may be more common geographically (reddish screech owls are rare in Florida), while sometimes an intermediate or brown phase is known. The tawny owl, the Eurasian counterpart of our barred owl, exhibits two phases in Great Britain, one being a cinnamon-brown, the other the tawny shade that gives the bird its name.

The rather somber feathering of owls precludes any displays of colorful plumes. In fact, since the sexes are indistinguishable or nearly so, a displaying male has no knowledge of whether he is attracting a female or repelling a rival male until he sees the reaction of the second bird. Head bobbing and weaving and body swaying enter into some owl displays, and bill snapping into most. Species that nest in open situations fly about the nest site in a form of aerial courtship, that of the snowy owl being merely a high-flying, circling flight, whereas the short-eared owl punctuates its stately cruising with the muffled sounds of its wings striking together.

Owls have a mutual respect for the strong, lethal talons each brandishes, and, apart from the nesting season, make sure they avoid warfare. In their anxiety to evade conflict, the territory of great horned owls is divided, not by a line, but by a buffer zone, into which neither will venture. The rule is arbitrarily suspended while mates are sought during the nesting season, the supplication of the female proclaiming her sex. The inherent animosity of the pair is gradually broken down until reciprocal head bobbing, billing and even cooing are reminiscent of the local drive-in theater. Food may be proffered by the male, the chief purpose of which is to divert the female from thoughts of cannibalism. The male cannily reasons that so long as she is digesting a toothsome meadow vole she will not consider dissecting him.

Because they do not migrate, the territory of an owl will be defended against others of the same kind throughout the year, with, of course, sufficient relaxation to permit two birds, one of each sex, to live in the same territory during the breeding season. Sometimes the belligerence may be extended to other kinds of owls with similar food habits, but as no two kinds have identical food tastes, some degree of tolerance may be expected.

Versatility in unmusical sounds is common to both sexes of some species and possibly to all, but as the duets, which are not uncommon, are usually given only at night, the proof is difficult to obtain. It is known that a number of species have a sort of Morse code among themselves. The number of deep-toned hoots of a great horned owl will determine the sex, the male's being the more numerous, but there may be some significance in the number given, which is inconsistent regardless of sex. It is when four, five or six owls fill the woods with their interpretation of operatic arias that the difference in tone and rhythm is so evident. The deep-toned calls can carry for long distances, yet seem no louder whether close at hand or far away; while all owl voices seem to have a ventriloquistic quality. Many of the smaller owls have a monotonous series of toots in which a pattern can be recognized, and each individual seems to have its own formula.

The variety of sounds made by the great horned, barred, barn and the two eared owls is so great as to suggest each has some meaning. If bees can convey knowledge through their "dancing," it is reasonable to believe that owls — and other birds — can make a similar transmission through sounds. The chuckles, snorts, whistles and sneezes some species emit must be an attempt to pass on information, but as no naturalist seems to have heard all the sounds attributed to one species, a relationship between call and subsequent action has not been surmised. Almost all owls have three to as many as eight distinct calls including the "love song"; and in some species, none of these calls is like that given by the young in the nest which, in addition to having a food call throughout their nestling stage at least, progress through a series of as many as five calls through adulthood. When hunger is acute, a young bird will scream its head off in a manner resminiscent of an unruly child having a tantrum.

Owls commence nesting at varying times but so gauge matters that the time the young demand the heaviest feeding will coincide with the period when most small birds and young rodents are available. For that reason, great horned owls, facing a lengthy nesting period, incubate in the subzero temperatures of February, the young hatching when nude trees and shrubbery provide little shelter for mice and rabbits and hunting is easier. Insect-eating owls follow a similar program, adjusting the nesting season accordingly.

Owls nest from below ground to close to the tops of the tallest trees. No one species seems to have a restricted site, although almost all have preferences with regard to the kind of tree and the location of the nest itself. Owls are, preeminently, hole-nesters, selecting natural cavities in trees or rocks and holes excavated by woodpeckers. The larger the owl the greater will be its difficulty in finding a suitable cavity and the greater the likelihood of its using a stick nest. No material is added to the cavity, whatever its origin, while the lining is of adventitious matter, such as feathers of victims or of the owl itself, along with remnants of meals. Those birds using stick nests are more inclined to make use of abandoned nests (crows, ravens, eagles, hawks, herons and the dreys of squirrels) rather than build their own. There have been instances where a pair of owls and a pair of hawks have alternated or rotated two or three nests made by the latter, but, again, the owls made no attempt at refurbishing. There are exceptions, of course. Some individuals will add a little lining and some will fashion a creditable stick nest. The great gray owl is quite adept at that sort of thing. The snowy, short-eared and marsh owls nest on the ground and, to contribute to inconsistency, so does the long-eared on occasion.

The screech owl has long been known to nest in man-made bird houses, designed either for itself or for the flicker. Recently, it has been discovered that the burrowing owl of the west is not averse to using a fabrication – this owl of subterranean inclination has been nesting on the shoulders of certain roads in California. Human activity has brought about the collapse of such nests, and when the plight of the owls was realized, naturalists shored the collapsed tunnels, where the chambers, at least partially artificial, were eagerly accepted by the owls. This is the owl that also uses the holes dug by prairie dogs, but not as a commune. The myth that prairie dogs, burrowing owls and prairie rattlesnakes share one dwelling as an harmonious triumvirate still prevails in some quarters.

The burrowing owl found in Florida is the same species as the one found in the west, although taxonomists rate it subspecifically distinct. This eastern form of the burrower really lives up to its name and digs its own caves. In recognition of its industry, if for nothing else, scientists might grant it full specific status. Indeed, it is surprising that it is not genetically distinct from the western form, as the two are separated by the Gulf of Mexico, Louisiana and half of Texas, although a family reunion may be held in winter when western birds drift southeast. The hub of the population of the Florida form is the geometric center of the state with the prairies occupying the Kissimmee region. From here, like spokes of a wheel, stragglers spread to almost all parts of the state.

The majority of owls have time for only one brood per year, as their calendar or nesting schedule is geared to certain non-repetitive events in the lives of mammals and other birds. Occasionally, however, the Eurasian little owl is two-brooded, while the almost cosmopolitan barn owl will, in certain localities and in good vole years, breed continuously, prudently reducing breeding to none in times of adversity.

Predatory birds and mammals, with owls heading the list, have long been practitioners of birth control, making the normal clutch difficult to determine, even within a species. This is particularly evident in northern climes, where the principal food may be voles, lemmings or hares, all subject to periodic cycles of abundance and scarcity. In exceptionally hard times, no nesting or, at least, egg-laying will take place. But if it is evident the food supply is in good quantity, the clutch will be two or even three times the average, although the great horned owl, whose strength and skill in hunting gives it a large choice of food, consistently lays but two eggs annually.

The shape of birds' eggs is governed by the relative size of the eggs laid and the kind of nest used. Eggs, which are large for the size of the bird are pointed and arranged (usually in the scantiest of nests) tips in, where they are more easily covered. The problem of users of open, fabricated nests is of packing within a restricted space, so that a certain but lesser degree of pyriformity follows. The great gray owl, which makes liberal use of stick nests, lays such eggs, but its two Continental cousins, the Ural and the tawny owls, both hole nesters, lay the round eggs of most owl species. This shape permits indiscriminate packing and even stacking, and is common to all birds that nest in holes.

With very few exceptions, eggs laid in nests in cavities are white, because there is no need for protective coloration. As even the ground-nesting owls lay white eggs, there is the suggestion that nesting on the ground by such species is comparatively recent. Owls' eggs vary in degree of gloss and smoothness, some being quite pitted or granulated.

There is an unequal relationship between the size of the owl and the size of its eggs. The eggs of the tiny elf owl measure two and one-half centimetres by two and one-half centimetres and are therefore about half the length and diameter of those of the great horned, which is almost five times as big.

Predatory birds are not obliged to hatch their young as quickly as others which strive to get their young out of reach of enemies as quickly as possible. The killdeer, robin and screech owl are all about the same length, about twenty-five centimetres, yet have eggs and incubation periods of varying duration. Young killdeer, capable of running about as soon as they hatch, undergo most of their development within the egg, which is larger than a robin's, whose young are quite helpless when born. Young screech owls, which have but few enemies, hatch from eggs of the same size as a robin's but which are incubated as long as a killdeer's.

The male owl rarely assists in incubation but, as with the hawks, assiduously brings food to, first, his mate, then to her and the young, finally assisting in their care when they have left the nest.

With the exception of the pygmy owls, all begin incubating as soons as the first egg is laid, bringing about a birth every day or so until, in the case of a large brood, the youngest and oldest differ considerably in development. As the birds hatch, the female owl must give more and more time to hunting. The incubation, which must continue nevertheless, is efficiently albeit inadvertently carried out by those owlets already out of the egg. This is an even greater help in such boreal species as the snowy and great horned owls, which nest when low temperatures prevail.

Young owls are born blind and thickly covered with a white or yellowish down, which is soon replaced by a second downy plumage even fluffier than the first. A most incongruous sight is that of a large owl tenderly holding up the head of a weakling in order to place food in its maw.

The young are fed the same sort of food consumed by their parents but are given the smaller and presumably more tender birds and mammals. The parents decapitate prey, consuming the heads themselves, and the young take the rest of the body in one gulp.

Later, the young are given the whole victim, whose head has been previously crushed. In time, whole mice, and then, if the owl is of a large species, rats and squirrels reach the owlets intact.

If food is abundant, or if the individual is overly zealous, an owl may supply the young with more food than they can eat, but this storage does not seem to be the result of foresight, nor does it fall into the definition of a cache. Both the Eurasian and North American pygmy owls will cache small mammals, but, like jays, will lose all recollection of the larder's location. Once, though, when in woods occupied by great horned owls, I found a cache I attributed to those birds. It was a neat pile of five meadow voles (one decapitated) and one deer mouse, lying on top of fresh snow in March. The bird could have been dropping mice in one spot because the young were not ready for such food. It is possible, too, that he may have approached the nest with a mouse, signalled his spouse accordingly and, failing to receive the correct or any response, may have elected to drop the bodies where he did. Ritual, beginning with the approach to courtship, plays no small part in the homelife of a bird.

Hatching as they do at intervals, there is invariably one owlet which, stronger than the rest, claims the greater share of food. Surprisingly though, a large number of runts survive, but not all. If the pangs of hunger overrule the consanguinity of bedmates, the larger owlets will turn on the smaller and weaker siblings, a seemingly harsh treatment but one which helps in the perpetuation of the species when food is in short supply. Nature deems it preferable that one survive rather than all starve.

Owls are just as unpredictable in the defence of the nest as are hawks. Where one or both of a pair of great horned owls will strike an intruder, another pair will steal quietly away. And the diminutive pygmy owl may attack more furiously than some particular great horned. The screech owl, which nests closer to human habitations than all except the barn owl, accounts for more attacks than any other, but in most cases, when a hat is knocked askew by a defence-minded bird it is attributed to ghosts, gremlins or a gust of wind. Nevertheless, as the talons are potentially dangerous, precautionary measures should be taken whenever a nest of any kind of owl is approached.

A young owl just out of the nest is an endearing bundle of fluff. When found on the ground, it can seem, and may be quite defenceless. And, because of its chittering or piteous crying, it may also seem to have lost all contact with its parents. In due course, however, one or both parents will appear with food. If they are tardy in making an appearance, the young one will seek cover or may even climb into a bush for greater safety. In any event, it should be left severely alone to ensure its proper and full development rather than subjecting it to the ill-advised care of a human.

Birds of prey swallow much indigestible matter, regurgitating or casting up such material, a practice more evident in owls because they are more inclined to bolt food entire. These ejections, or pellets, are a tightly and neatly rolled cylindrical mass, velvety in texture, consisting of hair and bones. Such roughage, while passing through most of the digestive system, is apparently essential to the well-being of the owl, as a captive little owl obtained relief by ingesting a quantity of elastic bands, ejecting them later along with the hard remains of insects. It has been found, too, that until the pellet is ejected, the owl is disinclined to eat.

Some kinds of owls repair to a favorite roost to consume their prey, remaining there during digestion. Pellets therefore accumulate in sometimes considerable quantities on the ground below, thus leading to the eventual discovery of the bird itself. And, of course, examination of those pellets by trained biologists give a complete story of the food of the bird.

Man has always been at such a disadvantage at night that he has always feared nocturnal creatures. Thus, while he would bravely face a towering mammoth or a thundering herd of bison by day, he shrank from meetings with night-prowling beasts like panthers. No doubt even the eye-shine of nocturnal animals induced terror, or, at least, belief in the supernatural. Owls, frequently heard, infrequently seen, birds whose lives were shrouded in mystery, were long ago endowed with the evil powers associated with creatures of the night. Superstitious beliefs are world-wide, or, at least, rampant wherever a truly nocturnal owl is found. Some are truly laughable, some pathetic, and it would require a second volume just to describe them fully.

Pitfalls of identification await any owl-watcher and I use as an example, an experi-ence of my own. On a cheerless November day, when my life list was a munificent seventy-five species or so, with ownership of binoculars still many moons away, I was afield in a local valley devoid of highrises, parking lots and pseudo-conservation areas, and was threading the leafless woods reviewing facts of the screech owl, a biography of which I had just read. And then I saw it.

Perched on a thick limb, about half way up a tree and a little distance from the trunk, it was facing me, ear tufts rivalling a pair of exclamation points, but eyes tightly shut in slumber. It was gray, and I wondered if a red companion were nearby. I began to circle it, with all the caution, all the finesse of an Indian stalking an enemy camp. Still it did not stir, did not even open an eye. I had completed an eighth of a circle, then ninety degrees, a little more – and then I could see the tail curved gracefully up the back as only a gray squirrel can hold it!

The accounts that follow are not of squirrels but of owls, companions, Roger Tory Peterson insists, of "Ghoulies and ghosties, and long-legged beasties, and things that go bump in the night."

The arrangement and nomenclature follows the Fifth Edition of the AOU Checklist, and subsequent supplements.

Barn Owl (*Tyto alba*)

Found in the southwestern tip of British Columbia and the southwestern corner of Ontario in Canada, and from or near the Canadian border south to the tip of South America (Amazon basin excepted); and throughout Europe, Africa (except the Sahara), the Middle East, southern Asia and Australia. Withdraws towards the equator in winter.

The barn owl, an individualist among raptors, has as many characteristics as the woodcock, one being to belie its name and show an impartiality toward barns. Its ancestral home was doubtless a cavity in a tree or fissure in a rock face, but all through the chronicles of man will be found evidence that this owl has shared his abode. It may be presumptuous, but I believe that the barn owl may have been an associate of those humans whose fossil remains were found in Pleistocene deposits in floors of Crimean caves. The reason for my belief is that the earliest remains of house mice were found there, too.

Man himself has no attraction for the bird, which is why it will nest apart from him, in holes in cliff banks, in the abandoned burrows of animals, the deserted nests of crows and, on occasion, even in barns; but it prefers the loft of an old building or a church steeple, because such edifices are usually located in a mouse- or rat-infested area.

Its selection of old, decrepit structures may explain why such buildings are often thought haunted, for a nest of barn owls can supply all the sound effects of an Alfred Hitchcock movie. Its repertoire includes rasping snores, a nighthawk-like *peent*, growls and rattles combined, snake-like hissing, a castenet-like snapping, right up to a shriek that would increase Dracula's pallor. Ghost-wise, it seems to omit only the clanking of chains.

Training for these off-stage sound effects begins early. The almost incessant whimper of the young ceases only when they make a temporary switch to the food-call, a sound greatly resembling that made by an uncouth person spooning soup. As the young mature, they progress through a high-pitched, quavering whine and a sibilant, throaty scream to a human-like shriek which, although shorter and higher than that of their parents, is every bit as blood-curdling.

The flight of this owl is an spectral as its voice. Moreover, the white or light underparts contribute to the effect of a ghostly apparition just as much as a sheet stolen from the clothesline. Add a wavering buoyancy, like a huge moth flying with deep wingbeats, sometimes even rocking from side to side, and one's belief in spirits is renewed, unless the characteristically trailing legs are seen, dispelling any notions of ghosts – or even moths.

While the barn owl commonly nests in old or deserted buildings, it does much hunting in open country – in the fields, marshes and meadows surrounding farms and small towns. It is not a wood- or forest-owl, but will hunt along roads traversing heavier tree growth and in open parkland grown with antiquated trees. If the latter is sprinkled with headstones, headlong flight by the observer usually ensues. In urban centers, it will frequent garbage dumps, granaries and those sections where the breeding of house mice and Norway rats proliferate in crowded, ancient buildings. In Australia, and no doubt elsewhere, it has a neat trick of flying past a hedge, flicking the growth with one wing. Small birds, settled for the night, make a hurried departure – and a meal for the owl.

Its heart-shaped face is very distinct from the round faces of other owls, while its ludicrous knock-kneed pose separates it from all except the burrowing owl, which also effects a bare-legged, stilt-like stance. Like the ephemeral spirits it emulates, the barn owl is never abroad by day except when clouds are very heavy. Usually it begins hunting in twilight, carrying on until dawn unless sated earlier or when the young are at their most demanding. In fact, it is so addicted to life after dark that, like the habitués of night-clubs, it seems bewildered in daylight and will strive to avoid direct sunlight.

Its predilection for the disease-spreading house rats and mice makes it one of our most valuable birds. Like other owls, it may occasionally vary its fare and sample large insects or a frog and may sometimes crowd human tolerance by capturing a small bird. As the rustle of a frog or bird in grass can differ little from that of a mouse, we can assume the catch was made in error.

So strongly nocturnal is this owl that it is an inveterate sleeper by day. Sometimes one found snoozing within a thickly foliaged tree or in the kind of cavity it chooses for nesting can be roused only with difficulty. It is rather unnerving to confront a barn owl at such a time, especially if the place is a musty attic, as the bird has a discomfiting habit of lowering its head and moving it from side to side, like the prelude to a charge by an infuriated bull.

In fall and winter, the solitary barn owl you have discovered may materialize into a dozen, for the birds roost communally at that time. Such conventions are enlarged by birds of northern origin, as this owl is one of the few that cannot adjust to cold weather. Although quitting the northern and southern extremities of its range in colder weather, it has the heron-like trait of wandering northward after nesting, in an attempt, perhaps, to effect a dispersal of young and therefore avoid inbreeding.

The male carries food to his mate and assiduously helps in the feeding of the young, but has a short attention span during the period of incubation. He may shirk the duty completely, may relieve his mate on occasion or even with regularity, and may even snuggle up cozily and incubate at the same time as she does. The barn owl, as stated at the beginning, is a bird of character.

Screech Owl (*Otus asio*)

Found from central British Columbia and a little north of the United States border elsewhere in Canada, south to central Mexico.

Hawks are not the only birds of prey with ridiculous misnomers. Owls come in for their share and the attractive little screech owl, appealing because of its small size, is saddled with a most glaring one. Screech it may, but E. H. Forbush seems to be the only reputable scientist to have heard it do so! Its commonly heard call is its love song and is the antithesis of a screech. It is a tremulous, quickly reiterated note that may be on one pitch throughout, may rise or fall toward the end, or may rise in the middle, falling back to, or near, the original pitch. It is a most un-owl-like sound, easily imitated, if one can reproduce its hollow quality, and is guaranteed to call up a flesh-and-blood screech owl. But it is not to be attempted unless the caller has strong nerves, for it is rather disconcerting to turn to find a screech owl has stolen up on ghostlike wings and is eyeing you with questionable intent from some nearby perch.

But it is a good sound to use if you are attempting to call up small birds, which take particular delight in mobbing a screech owl trying to recuperate its powers in sleep. Obviously, screech owls themselves will not respond unless you are in screech owl habitat which is a patch of open woods of reasonable size. A much favored locality is an old orchard of neglected apple trees abounding in cavities. And if a brook is nearby it is considered a preferred residential area in screech owl circles. An acceptable abode will be abandoned only temporarily, either through death or the yielding of one bird to the wishes of its mate, who might opt for another woodlot. In either event, some other screech owl may soon take over the broken lease.

This owl will occasionally take advantage of nest boxes erected for its use. As it must, perforce, use any cavity nature has provided, the quality of workmanship need not be extravagant. An entrance of seven centimetres is a requisite, apparently, as one made several ineffectual attempts to enter my purple martin house with its six centimetre openings.

Poor hunting, of course, will drive the birds farther afield, to farms and hedgerows where mice, rats or small birds are more numerous. A feeding station near an evergreen windbreak may mean the disappearance of a few small birds, a fact which may go unnoticed, as the screech owl hunts in darkness, or at least when light is dim, such as very early morning or late in the day. A sometime taste for fish will send it to openings in ice-bound waters where it will swoop across the hole to clutch a fish near the surface.

If you do chance upon a screech owl, it may feign sleep. I once found one five metres up in a tree, eyes apparently tightly closed. Moving some distance to one side, I found the bird still facing me, although I could not see its eyes. Then I moved directly back of it and its head twisted completely around. It could only have been watching me through yellow eyes reduced to mere slits.

When fully aware that it has been discovered, it will elongate its body, draw in its feathers and stretch its ear-tufts to the utmost. The effect is like a broken stub of a tree, a capital illusion if the "break" is where it should be, but a sorry one when it looks like a jagged stump protruding from the middle of a small branch. Still, the camouflage is so perfect that it is quite possible many screech owls are seen but not recognized as such by humans. One autumn day, before leaf fall, I was intrigued by a rectangular light patch well up a slender willow, tight against its trunk. I investigated further, not because I thought it was a bird, but because I could not imagine what sort of object would be away up there. It proved to be a slumbering screech owl, its back to me. It was presumably a favorite roost, as the bird was there the following day, more recognizable this time because it was now facing me.

A screech owl will also roost in the same type of hole it uses for nesting, sometimes utilizing the nest cavity itself. Back of the museum building in Toronto, Ontario was a tree containing such an opening and where, for a brief period for several successive winters, a screech owl would soak up January sunshine like any tourist in Florida. Sometimes one bird will share the roost with another which is in all likelihood its mate. There is a strong measure of safety precautions involved in seeking the seclusion of such

recesses during periods of inactivity. A field companion and I watched a frenzied kestrel try to reach an imperturbable screech owl cozily ensconced within a support of a steel truss bridge, three sides of which were solid, the fourth, the bottom one, open lattice work.

The presence of humans about its nest or even roost is not encouraged, as I found out one dark evening when I visited my office, which was then reached up a narrow driveway between two buildings. When your hat is knocked askew by an unseen assailant that travels on soundless wings, belief in the supernatural is bound to resurface. But when blood has been drawn, it is evident that the little demon was not some ectoplasm but a thing of substance, like a screech owl.

The screech owl, a species widely celebrated for its dichromatic plumage, is either grayish or reddish in its general tone. The different coloration follows no formula, although a few of its many races, particularly those of the southwest, are rarely seen in a reddish phase.

Great Horned Owl (*Bubo virginianus*)

Found from the tree limit in Alaska and Canada south to the tip of South America, including the Caribbean islands.

It was a night in late September. The tumult of a severe thunderstorm had disturbed those wishing to sleep in the first hour or so after midnight. Then the great god Thor banged more steel drums some time after daybreak. In between, torrents of rain fell. Nevertheless, I was out, bright-eyed and early, the next morning, dividing my time between looking for puddles on the trail and fall migrants in the trees, all the while cautiously detouring damp boughs heavy with moisture. Then I became aware that a black ash had sprouted a growth since my last trip down the valley. Binoculars came into play but it was some little time before I realized I was not looking at a cancerous deformity but a bedraggled and disconsolate great horned owl, morosely viewing the world through rain-rimmed eyes. It was so disgusted with its lot it gave scant attention to me as I passed. The trail ended in a cul-de-sac a little beyond, requiring me to retrace my route to a point where I could climb out of the valley. I was again approaching the owl, but now from the other direction. And found it with its wings outspread, drying in cormorant fashion!

The great horned owl is not our largest, being shaded by a fully feathered, great gray owl. In the nude, a de-feathered great gray is much the smaller. But the horned is our most powerful and most ferocious, fully deserving the name "eagle owl" applied to its Eurasian counterpart.

Varying hares and ptarmigan in the north and cottontails in the south comprise its principal bill of fare, but the pangs of acute hunger will precipitate an attack on any bird or medium-sized mammal. Pheasants and even swans have been assaulted. Wood-chucks by day, domestic cats by night, skunks with impunity and porcupines without, will do when hares are scarce. As birds are thought to have no sense of smell, the great horned may not be offended when sprayed by a skunk. On the other hand, in Canada's forbidding northeast, a horned owl tore into a sack containing bird specimens, fairly conclusive evidence that it was guided by its nostrils, not its eyes.

As befitting its size, the great horned is a bird of the heavy timber, although it will insist on the proximity of fields, marshes, meadows and similar open country for hunting. Its size, too, renders it the owl most frequently seen, although it is averse to courting detection. Many winter observations are made in sparsely grown, almost residential districts, where cover is provided by a few thick evergreens. It was in such a locality I saw one the day before writing this piece. The upper end of Toronto's High Park hosted a great horned most winters, much to the chagrin of rats that patrolled the animal enclosures by night. Persecution has had the effect of making it a very wary bird. Once it is aware of even the most innocuous individual, such as an owl-watcher, it will leave the ultimate in secluded roosts. Even a sharp sound may drive it from cover. As I am incapable of emitting a piercing whistle, I normally call my dog by clapping my hands, once breaking off in astonishment to follow the silent flight of a great horned I had startled into motion.

Another effortless way to owl-watch is to let vociferous crows or small birds like chickadees guide you to a hidden owl. If you are unable to see the bird, just curb your patience. The mobbing will force the owl to change its roost more than once as it seeks deeper cover.

The great horned embodies all the human conceptions of an owl: Great size and strength, large and fierce yellow orbs, a predilection for nocturnal activity and an utterance described as a hoot. In the still of the night, when its deep-toned, resonant *whoos* proceed from the depths of some gloomy, mysterious and otherwise silent woods, there is the urge to sit closer together, or to throw another log on the fire. Yet its call can sound like so many other things: A muted foghorn, the whistle of a distant steam locomotive, the bay of a hound. And if the bird is near, a ventriloquistic effect will transform it into the gentle cooing of a dove! The call of the male is of four or five notes, that of the female, six to eight. The only other owl giving a comparable hoot is the barred, whose call is normally of two groups of four notes each. The hooting of the great horned has a variety of purposes. One can stretch a point and call it a love song, but

in essence, it is the way one owl tells another to trespass only at great risk. It is also an invitation to a female to enter the territory of a male, after she first announces her sex, which she does by hooting her longer call. Very often, a male and a receptive female will engage in an antiphonal duet leading a human listener to believe the woods are occupied by a large flock of owls when all the while there are just two birds pitching a little whoo.

The captivation of the opposite sex produces bizarre performances throughout the animal world, with the great horned owl's displays no exception. The male drops his usually terrifying demeanor and will bow, ludicrously, to the female, following which he will stroke her with his bill, touch his bill to hers or even tender a dietary offering. Then, stretching his head high, he will swing it in a semicircle until it nears his feet, continuing on up to the other side to the zenith again, the owl equivalent of Tom Sawyer walking on his hands. The male owl is fully hooked when the female joins him in a bit of a dance.

Rarely does the female lay eggs in a structure of her own making, claiming, instead, an abandoned nest of crow, raven, hawk, heron or even squirrel, using the same one for three or four years before moving on. It may become quite a garbage heap in time, as the great horned's success in hunting outstrips the appetite of the family. Eighteen pounds of unused food were found at one nest.

Snowy Owl (*Nyctea scandiaca*)

Circumpolar. Found on the Arctic tundra, irregularly wintering south to the northern tier of states in the United States and occasionally as far south as the Gulf of Mexico. In the eastern hemisphere, not apt to cross the cordillera.

S nowy owl. Neighbor of the Eskimo, who named it ookpikjuak. Darling of the souvenir stands, whose proprietors rechristened it the more manageable ookpik.
The bird is prominent in Eskimo culture, as it is, among other things, a highly esteemed item of food. And the Eskimo's version of sun- or snow-glasses, narrow slits cut into a thin shield of bone, may have evolved from their observations of this owl which, like other owls, will narrow its eyes in strong light. The Eskimos also have a Munchausian-like legend that once such an owl caught two hares, one in each foot. The mammals, inextricably snared, took off in different directions. It makes for a ripping conclusion.

The snowy owl is so obviously a bird of the Arctic that one may wonder why it is included in a popular work such as this. This owl, however, is a sometime winter visitor to settled regions. For reasons only imperfectly understood, certain rodents and lagamorphs, the lemming and Arctic hare among them, have an oscillating abundance cycle, building up every few years to an unwieldy population. The ensuing crash greatly affects the economy of the snowy owl, which finds its preferred food, lemming or hare, in short supply. The alternative is to migrate southward to where the pastures are, if not greener, at least mouse-brown. While a few snowys will come south every winter, the periodicity of their appearance in large numbers is every four or five years, greatest when the populations of lemming and hare plummet at the same time. In the winter of 1901-02, from 500 to 1,000 birds were shot in Ontario alone, mortalities that would not occur today as the bird is protected from all except the ignorant and uncaring.

It is deplorable that, "trophy hunters" still enlarge their egos by illegally bagging the snowy, a curiosity wherever found, which, in winter, will be as far south as Latitude 40°, which stretches from Cape May, New Jersey, to Cape Mendocino, California, passing through Indianapolis and Denver on the way. The unsuspicious birds find life less hazardous in the sparsely settled midwest than in the east, where, because of the higher incidence of owl-spotters, it is reported more frequently.

Any creature whose home is the flat, monotonous expanse of the Arctic tundra, where each hillock of grass assumes the prominence of an Everest, will have little experience with trees. Thus, snowy owls visiting the south habitually perch on stumps, rocks, hayricks, seawalls or any slight eminence on the ground. When looking over snow-covered fields, short-grass meadows or marshes, or wide beaches, it is well to give careful scrutiny to a shapeless white lump. It may not be a stone or clump of grass topped with winter's coverlet. It may be a snowy owl. They often make use of the sloping roof of a barn or similar structure. Before it was ravaged by fire many years ago, the roof of the Palace Pier, an amusement center hard by Toronto's Sunnyside Beach, was a favored vantage point of a snowy fancying a duck dinner. After the holocaust, snowys made the seawall their launching pad.

From the foregoing, the notion will prevail that the snowy never perches in trees, but I saw one atop a transformer on a pole which, of course, is flat on top; and another sprawled over an apple tree. This latter bird may have found it difficult to balance on the slender twigs and was spread out on that account, but may also have been protecting food. Snowys do not cache the remnants of a kill but spend time between meals resting on top of it to protect it from thieving scavengers and to conserve it for future consumption. Moreover, my wife and I saw one bird perfectly at ease near the top of a tall, dead elm, evidence that perching is not an unknown art in the species.

Airlines would be happier if the birds confined their roosting to trees, because their use of the level expanse in an airport can and has led to serious plane crashes. But as planes receive the same legal protection as do the birds, the only solution to the problem seems to be trapping the owls and moving them elsewhere, a practice carried out at a few airports.

It is unfortunate that this owl confines its courting as well as its cries to the north, for few birds are more ludicrous to watch. The male seems so intent on having both first and last words, he apparently tries to deafen his mate so that she cannot hear him and therefore will not answer back. He HOOTS in capital letters, each booming note

accompanied by violent bows, while in between each he will execute an awkward little jig. The whole is a show of exuberance not in keeping with the bird's usually phlegmatic disposition. It has other calls when in the Arctic but the only one heard in the south, and that infrequently, is a raven-like croak.

The nest, if such it may be called, is little more than a hollow scraped out of a mound, unless the hen selects a rocky ledge on which she will place just sufficient material to keep the eggs from rolling off. And in all probability, most of the matter will already have been there.

Nesting on the ground in such an exposed situation requires constant vigil. In addition, uncovered eggs will chill quickly in the Arctic air. The female is therefore required to sit closely and almost constantly, her mate either on guard or hunting for the food he brings to the nest, at first for his mate only, later for both her and the young. She, however, is an accomplished huntress, in time contributing just as heavily to the larder as her spouse.

Your intrusion during the earlier stages of nesting will initiate not the expected broken-wing ruse of so many birds, but a rolling waddle as the hen engages in a promenade. Sometimes she will lie prone and whine like a cringing supplicant. If these histrionics prove ineffective, the male may attack, being careful, however, not to strike anything. The whole is a ridiculous performance by a bird of prey.

Hawk Owl (*Surnia ulula*)

Found in the coniferous forests throughout the northern hemisphere, although almost entirely absent from British Columbia. Occasionally winters to the south, in the western hemisphere to the uppermost tier of states in United States.

At one time, when ornithologists considered that hawks and owls were very much more closely related than they do now, the hawk owl was cited as the connecting link between the two groups. Many facets of its appearance and habits seemed to support the erroneous theory.

Its facial disc is somewhat imperfect, imparting a physiogomy less flat than that of other owls; and it has an uncharacteristically long tail. When perched on a dead stub or other commanding position, it will raise that appendage, then lower it slowly like a hermit thrush or a lethargic kestrel. It will even hover like the latter bird. Its appearance in flight may approach that of a dark and noiseless goshawk or, if size is hard to determine as it dodges about low growth, it may suggest a sharp-shinned hawk. If the long tail escapes notice, the bird may seem like a dark pigeon. In habits, it is very, but not entirely diurnal, and perches with a slight inclination of the body, like a hawk, rather than in the mid-Victorian upright posture of other owls. Its long tail enables it to thread trees with the ease of an accipiter, but no hawk or fellow owl will perch with the tail held at a jaunty angle.

In its hunting, it combines certain habits of the accipiters and the shrikes. Watching from some vantage point overlooking a burnt-over tract or at the edge of a brushy opening in the forest, it will drop low and flap and sail across the open, perhaps stopping for a few seconds on the top of one or two low bushes within the enclosure. Reaching the far edge, it will swoop upwards, shrikelike, to another perch. Should prey be sighted during its aerial reconnaissance it will drop to the ground, picking up a mouse, lemming or ground squirrel. In winter the victim may be a ptarmigan or grouse.

From February through April, the male becomes aware that hawk owls come in two sexes and that it might be expedient to stake out a territory and attract a mate. A melodious and tremulous whistled trill, sounding like *wita wita wite*, is his epithalamium; but of his several other calls, only a hawklike chatter may be heard during its infrequent irruptions to the south.

When the nest is as low as two metres from the ground, its examination presents only one problem. Both birds object so vigorously to the inspection that the investigator may find himself sporting a few lacerations. When the nest is higher up, the problems are compounded. The most popular site is within the top of a broken stub or trunk perhaps ten metres up, and as such trees may be in the last stages of decay, to climb them is to invite serious injury. Sometimes the owl is attracted to a tree cavity with a side entrance, whether the opening is a natural one or one prepared by a flicker or pileated woodpecker. Occasionally it will make use of a crow's old nest.

The hawk owl presents little opportunity for study except to those intrepid ornithologists who dare enter its northern home. There, one must be prepared to battle through clouds of insects or deep snow, while stumbling through tamarack and spruce swamps, over treacherous muskeg or through scarcely penetrable thickets of alder or aspen.

One saved me such an arduous safari by flying across the sunlit river at Eau Claire, Ontario, where it would be on the southern fringe of its range. Dr. E. L. Brereton, a reputable and respected naturalist, now deceased, reported to me that he thought he had seen one near Huntsville, Ontario, one August day, an even more southern location. Another observer, David Reynolds of Ottawa, picked up what he thought was a road fatality near that Ontario city in June. He carried the presumably dead bird in his car until he reached his destination, left it on a stump for some ten minutes, and then set about burying it. A regretable and final stroking of its beautiful feathers preceded the actual interment, an act never consummated. The owl left the graveside like a shot. Reynolds thought he had seen the bird blink once while in his car but was unable to detect signs of life otherwise. At no time did he feel he was being scrutinized by a living bird, although he was aware of being continually transfixed by a stare of utmost malevolence and loathing.

The irruptions of the hawk owl, unlike those of the snowy, are very few and far between, and are quite unpredictable. The last was during the winter of 1962-63, when

unprecedented numbers came south to the delight of birders in parts of southern Canada and the northern United States. As many as ten were found within Metropolitan Toronto, while more took up temporary abode in the area surrounding the city. My thoughts, when I found one with a vole dangling from its beak, were: "What a long journey just to go mousing!" Still, we birders will travel farther for a "lifer."

But, without straying far from home, that particular invasion enabled a good many naturalists to better the exploits of Audubon who, for all his far-flung travels, never saw a hawk owl in his lifetime.

Barred Owl (*Strix varia*)

Found east of the Rocky Mountains and the Great Plains from northern British Columbia and the Maritime Provinces south almost to Panama. There is evidence that it is moving westward into the range of the related spotted owl.

The first and almost every subsequent intimate meeting with a barred owl elicits a feeling akin to pity. With its round, dark eyes set in a grayish facial disc, the bird looks as if it had been the loser in some altercation, acquiring two dandy shiners in the process.

This owl, though fairly large, is not as strong as its size suggests. Its relatively weak talons restrict it to victimizing only small mammals and birds. It ranks as one of our better mousers and, if devotees of Noah Webster raise no objection, ratters. Only diseased and crippled chickens and game birds will be captured by the barred owl.

The barred and the great horned are hooting owls and are the two most frequently heard. If you have been unable to reconcile their differences, just remember that the barred owl is sometimes called "eight-hooter," hooting with a rythm something like a locomotive whistling for a crossing. The call is in two groups of four, WHOO-WHOO, TO-WHOO; WHOO-WHOO, TO-WHOO. On paper, it resembles the wheels of the rolling stock trailing a locomotive, but the graph should show the wheels of the caboose slipping off the track into the ditch below, as the final WHOO slides well down the scale. Other barred owls will answer from near and far until one feels as if in the midst of a railroad yard. Sometimes the interspersed deeper hoots of a great horned will signal something amiss with the "railway system."

But that is just the beginning. Let two eight-hooters meet in some Stygian rendez-vous and the night will be attended by a greater variety of noises than can be produced by all of catdom. There will be hoots, of course, but also screams, coos, chuckles and sounds close to belly laughs. If the performers become aware of an audience, all calls will cease and a silence as profound as the surrounding darkness will descend on the stage. Then, just as suddenly as it stopped, it will start again – but this time right over your head, the birds having floated in on soundless wings.

Near sunset one July day, I caught an interesting couple in a high and dry maple bush. The two were so lightly colored I suspected they were birds of the year, which may have explained the absence of some of the more terrifying notes associated with this species. But variety was still there, with each medley ending in an undignified burp. During the concert, I was impressed by their very deliberate, parrot-like movements. Although the bill was not used in climbing, the toes grasped the limb with all the precision of a macaw's.

Had it been earlier in the season and had the two been adult male and female, the caterwauling would have been accompanied by ridiculous postures and attitudes, with the birds bobbing and bowing with half-spread wings. Heads would have been turned this way and that, sometimes with such a wobble as to suggest insecure mounting.

The flight of the larger great horned is quite soundless but falls short of the eerie progress of the barred whose slow wingbeats carry it through the woods like a brown specter. The bird will slip and skim through and around branches with all the grace of a swallow. Then, nearing its perch, it will curve upwards in a long glide.

As both barred and great horned are owls of the woods, both will inhabit the same tract if it is large enough. The barred, though, will keep to the ridges, the other to the lower, swampy ground, an area the barred is not averse to using if it can manage to lay claim to it. In fact, its ideal habitat will also include three gloomy spots, one for nesting, one for roosting and one for feeding, with some water at hand for drinking and bathing. Much of its hunting, of course, is not in the woods themselves, but over fields and about farms. Sedentary by preference, the birds in the northern part of the species' range are forced southward only if their food supply fails in winter. At such times they will enter towns and cities, keeping to the older, well-treed parts where rats and mice like to congregate and where the birds will find cover. Indeed, the farther one travels south in eastern United States, the easier it becomes to find barred owls. They are rated the most common member of the order in Florida and Texas, where they are not only more abundant but more easily seen, thanks to the scarcity of the large, thick trees they seek for shelter in the north.

Although the barred owl avoids all meetings with the great horned, it is quite indifferent to the red-shouldered hawk, whose tastes in food and wooded areas is almost identical. Naturally, as only one species works the graveyard shift, there is no conflict at the table. As the hawk ordinarily has two nests, using each in alternate years,

the owl sees to it that the one currently in disfavor does not remain idle. And misreading the calendar has resulted in their sharing the same nest – for a short while, anyway.

Failing to find an untenanted red-shoulder's nest, the owl will seek a cavity in a tree and, as a last recourse, will use a stick nest of its own construction. This, however, is a shoddy affair that either of the first two little pigs could better. It is so poorly constructed that the exercising by the young and the comings and goings by the parents soon have the nest awry. In fact, the young have been known to fall out. Huffing and puffing would reduce it to shambles faster than any house of straw built by pigs.

The barred owl is often easily found, and still more often called up by one who can imitate either its call or the squeak of a mouse. Faint-hearts should not attempt this gambit as just as a cacaphonious pair will startle the daylights out of you, so will a curious, solitary one. It may answer from afar for a while and then, on those incredibly silent wings, will drift in to a perch back of you and still your heart with a sudden *"Boo-boo, to-you! Boo-boo, to-you-all!"*

Great Gray Owl (*Strix nebulosa*)

In North America found west of Quebec and Wisconsin, from the tree line south to Lake Superior in the east, the northern tier of states centrally and down the cordillera to northern California in the west; and from the tree line in Eurasia south to the cordillera. In winter, occasionally moves up to 200 kilometres south.

If the Province of Ontario were to choose something in feathers to accompany its floral emblem, the white trillium, it might give serious consideration to the great gray owl. This is one of the few birds the province can claim as its very own. The specimen on which Johann Reinhold Forster based his original description for science was obtained near the mouth of the Severn River, on Hudson Bay, in 1772. Unfortunately, the province shares the species with western Canada, Alaska, Russia, Scandinavia and mountainous United States, for it is a wide-ranging bird of the far north. Its summer occurrence east of Hudson Bay is doubtful.

This is the largest owl in the world, at least fifteen centimetres longer than any other. But strip it of feathers and the nude body is scarcely bigger than that of its close relative, the barred owl. A proportionately long tail and lax, softer and more numerous feathers contribute to its greater length and bulk.

Yet its soft, dense feathering aids it little in flight which, while noiseless, is heavy and labored, lacking the buoyancy of the barred owl. It glides a great deal, like that bird, swooping up to a perch in much the same manner. But its flight is usually closer to the ground, while its steering is almost entirely by its tail. Laborious though it may seem in the air, there is nothing ungainly in the way it will check its progress and dexterously drop on a mouse.

Few people are able to see this owl in action, for its home is the awkwardly negotiated muskeg, the thick, northern forests of pine, spruce and tamarack, and the timbered slopes of the mountainous west. There it will have two favorite roosts, one for nesting, one for dining, sometimes combining the two into a bed-sitting room.

The members of this genus are more given to nest building than are other owls, but only the great gray makes a habit of it, using sticks and even adding the luxury of a lining in the way of feathers and the hair of deer and moose. As a nest builder, the great gray is no oriole, although its structures are an improvement on those of the mourning dove and black-billed cuckoo, which sometimes fail to hold a newly laid egg. If the owl has a larger or more vigorous brood than usual or if the parents are required to make too many trips to the nest, babies, cradle and all take a tumble.

Nest building cannot be an ingrained habit, as some birds continue to use the abandoned nests of crows and of gos, red-tailed and broad-winged hawks, only one of which regularly shares its breeding range. Perhaps its nest-building proclivities have arisen from the shortage of old nests to be found within the taiga, just as it must forego the comfort of nesting within a cavity, as the taiga contains few trees of a diameter sufficient to accommodate the bulk of a great gray owl.

The male wants none of the duties of incubation, although he considerately and promptly brings food to his sitting mate, who advises him of her hunger by a loud call. As he approaches the nest, he will hoot softly, with his mouth full, having stopped en route to transfer the mouse from feet to bill.

Nor does the pair seek warlike encounters, allowing nest and contents to be examined with impunity. True, the distress call of the young, whether in or out of the nest, will transform the female into a feathered fury, with as little disregard for her well-being as a football lineman has for his. Few people take advantage of this normally tractable nature as the climb up a slender fifteen metre spruce or tamarack, in which the nest may be situated, is a hazard in itself.

The great gray owl has the usual variety of soft calls when about the nest but has two calls more noteworthy. One, matching its great bulk, is a booming, evenly spaced hooting, the pitch of each hoot falling at the end, something like the drop in the last note of the barred. The other, in keeping with the small size of its de-feathered body, is a vibrant, wavering sound resembling the quaver of the little screech owl.

The great gray is so tame and so inoffensive and gentle that it has been caught by hand. But one could scarcely expect a savage nature in a bird whose prey, in summer at least, is nothing but mice, the capture of which requires not even a threatening gesture. In winter it might supplement that diet with northern finches, such as redpolls, siskins and crossbills.

Failing food supplies brought about by deep snow and other factors will force the

species southward, but its irruptions know no cycle nor are they as spectacular as those of the snowy owl, its neighbor to the north. Flights occurred in 1889-90, 1907 and 1950-51. In the latter period, thirty-six specimens reached a taxidermist in Swastika, Northern Ontario. In 1965-66 a minor influx deposited one at Huntsville, 300 kilometres farther south. This bird was viewed and photographed by so many people during the two days it remained on exhibition that it is surprising some local entrepreneur did not take advantage of the opportunity to inaugurate yet another money-raising event.

It is unlikely that North America will again see an invasion of great grays equal to that of the winter of 1978-79. The invasion was carried out on such a wide front it seemed that every great gray owl in northern Canada moved south to some degree, with the more venturesome becoming the cynosures of all binoculars from New York and New England west across the northern two tiers of states. Possibly as a result of invasions such as have been experienced in the last couple of decades, great gray owls became established in the fir forests of Yosemite Valley back in 1915. A similar isolated homestead was reported from northern Minnesota in 1935.

Owls of any kind are so rarely seen that one, when found, will soon be surrounded by the curious, who will not be restricted to confirmed bird-watchers. The attraction of the great gray is no less than that of the boreal and hawk owls, because the presence of any of the three in the settled parts of the country is a very rare and unexpected event. Rare-bird alerts and the grapevine, both organized and confused, will soon have a befuddled owl surrounded by binoculars and cameras. His wide-staring yellow eyes regard the observers with supreme indifference. Only when the clicking shutter is poked a shade too close does the owl reply in kind — a fretful snapping of the mandibles.

Long-eared Owl (*Asio otus*)

Summers from near the tree line in Alaska and Canada south to, roughly, a line connecting the southernmost parts of California and Virginia; and in Eurasia from about the Arctic Circle south to about Latitude 30°N. In North America, winters south to Baja, California and central Mexico.

If it is your pleasure to see a long-eared owl, then search regions of heavy coniferous growth seeking therein an upright branch broken jaggedly about twenty-five centimetres above its union with a horizontal limb. Then scrutinize it carefully to determine if it is a bird or branch, for the long-ear mimics such a fractured stem to perfection. Ordinarily, its feathers are fluffed out and lax; but if danger is thought imminent, it will draw them in, stretch its vertically held body, point its centrally located ear-tufts to the zenith and close its eyes to mere slits. This creates such an artful deception that your eyes will give it but a passing glance; unless, however, the broken stub has the incongruity of being bigger in diameter than the parent branch.

Two long-ears I surprised in a tangle of pussy willow showed how instinctive the reaction is. No stub five to ten centimetres in diameter will be found on a stem about the thickness of a finger! Yet the two birds repeatedly tried the simulation as I flushed them from one spot to another. Even in flight their intent was to deceive. When the long-eared owl spreads its wings and takes to the air, the forty-centimetre bird metamorphoses into a Boeing 747, so broad are the wings. Two major differences are apparent in this transfiguration. The owl floats as silently as thistle-down. And where the jet climbs in direct flight, the owl wavers, flutters and hovers like a huge Mesozoic brown moth, whose destination is as vague as a paper kite's in a vagrant breeze.

The flight of its close relative, the short-eared owl, is much the same, and both display the same under-wing markings. There the similarity of the two ends. The long-ear is not a marsh owl but a forest one, preferring thick conifers or even deciduous woods, either growth adjacent to the open country it will hunt over. Swamps of tamarack, cedar and alder and the impassable, small mixed growth that sometimes borders lakes and streams also attract it. Nor can you expect to see it abroad by day as you can the short-ear. The long-ear restricts its activities to the dusk of early morning or late evening, unless the moon is high or the day has an exceptional overcast.

Even the "ears" differ. The ear-tufts of both sprout from near the center of the head but are conspicuously flaunted by the long-ear, imparting a cat-like appearance when the bird is alert. Those of the short-ear are so small and so concealed by the feathers of the head as to suggest nothing more than mere bumps on the cranium. Still, there is something feline about the appearance of the short-ear too, but, because of the tiny ears, the appearance is more that of a kitten.

Not only is it unlikely you will see long-ears and short-ears at the same time or place, you will not find a long-ear if a great horned is around, as the two are quite incompatible.

Both eared owls are renowned for their ceaseless warfare on mice. Almost 80 per cent of the long-ear's food consists of injurious rodents, which are pounced upon after a long, silent glide. The few small birds it takes are caught in the same way, the birds revealing their location on some nocturnal perch by stirring restlessly.

The long-ear nests from the ground to as high as fifteen metres up. Ground and near-ground nests are self-built affairs of sticks and lining. But the owl will also nest higher, remodelling slightly the rim and lining of old structures architectured by crows, hawks, herons or squirrels. A cavity will do in a pinch.

The long-ear's varied vocabulary will be heard only about its nest. A soft, mellow hooting, reminiscent of the coo of a dove, is its song. Excited birds will call *kwek-kwek-kwek*, compared by some authors to the call of a very alarmed duck, but which, to me, sounds like the frenzied cawing of a crow, but less raucous. The calls of the male to the occupants of the nest sounds like the muffled *whoofs* of a dog.

Examination of its nest can be conducted with singular safety and surprising results. The female will use a broken-wing ruse as good as any enacted by a killdeer, adding, however, a catlike mewing. If such histrionics prove ineffective, one of the birds will simulate the capture of some prey, even including a passable imitation of the victim's expiring cries.

Long-ears are most conspicuous in February, the mating season and November, when from a handful to as many as fifty will be found frequenting a cluster of

146

evergreens adjacent to good hunting territory. Such a gathering will be the amalgamation of several families and occurs not from the desire for convivial companionship but from a common interest in the abundant rodent life to be found in the nearby fields. The owls, however, will be on a migration trek at this time, which may take them as far south as Mexico, Texas and Florida, for both eared owls are inclined to winter in more equitable climes. One long-ear, banded in San Diego, California, was recaptured in North Bay, Ontario, evidence that owls, as a group, are not as sedentary as supposed.

Short-eared Owl (*Asio flammeus*)

In the western hemisphere found from the Arctic Ocean south to a line connecting the southernmost parts of California and Virginia; from the base of the bulge in South America to its tip; and in Colombia, Ecuador, Hawaii, Galapagos and some Caribbean islands; in the western hemisphere from or near the Arctic ocean south to the latitude of the Mediterranean Sea. Withdraws from the northernmost parts of its range in winter.

In late December of 1962, seventeen short-eared owls descended on a large farm field a little west of Toronto, remaining there for the balance of the winter. My wife and I made frequent visits to the area, sitting quietly in the car while the broad-winged birds floated about, resembling a gathering of moths. Long before we reached the venue of the winter convention, occasional air-borne individuals could be seen. Once within the convention hall, the air would be filled with their disturbed forms, all flitting about aimlessly, their deep, easy wing-beats graceful, yet, at the same time, flapping quite unlike those of any other owl except the closely allied long-ear. The birds would rise from, and resettle on fence posts, stumps, rocks, even the ground, points of vantage in awaiting the reappearance of a meadow vole, for it was the abundance of that rodent that summoned the conclave. Similar but slightly smaller caucases were held in the same general region in the second and fifth winters following.

The short-ear will gather in mouse- and lemming-infested areas to an even greater degree than will the long-ear. Gatherings of up to hundreds have occurred in England, South America, Canada, the Scandinavian countries and even Scotland, where the species had previously been almost unknown. Some years ago, C. E. Hope, of the Royal Ontario Museum, examined 1078 pellets of short-eared owls collected at Toronto, finding them to contain the remains of 1181 meadow voles, 450 deer mice, one house mouse, eight snow buntings, two house sparrows and one horned lark. The remains of four other birds could not be identified.

The preponderance of rodents, especially voles, is sufficient indication that the birds were attracted to the superabundance of those mammals, confirming studies made elsewhere. Yet the birds cannot expect a cenotaph in their memory. About one hundred years ago, short-ears decimated a colony of terns. And in the winter of 1909-10, they preyed exclusively on small birds wintering at Toronto's Ashbridge's Bay, even though the place was creeping with voles, according to J. A. Munro, who witnessed their fall from grace.

Short-ears also hunt in the quartering fashion of a harrier, even duplicating the dihedral to a small degree; or they may hover, like a rough-legged hawk, dropping down to clutch some luckless mouse with piercing talons.

Such aerial activities are nothing compared to the courtship flight of the male. This is performed high above the nest site, usually when light is poor, and consists of flapping and soaring in broad circles to the accompaniment of one of his more common notes, which may be repeated up to twenty times. He will break off to go into his wing-clapping routine, striking the tips of his primaries below the body while making a slanting dive. Then he will swoop upward to recommence his circling. In essence, the sound produced by his wings is not a clap but a whispered fluttering, a soft-shoe rather than a tap dance. There is an intriguing similarity between this display, with its accompanying call, and the booming power dive and nasal *peent* of the nighthawk, a member of that group of birds to which owls seem to have some relationship.

The short-ear's version of the Indian love call is a series of notes, usually in triplets, interpreted by others as *waks* or *yaks*. If the female makes no response, the sequence may be reduced to one prolonged *w-a-a-c-k*. Since the call strikes my ear as *itch, itch, itch,* the note of annoyance becomes one long *i-t-c-h.* There is also an emphatic call, a combination of a bark and an explosive sneeze which, in the modern vernacular, may be expressed as, *like, Wow!* Few of these calls will be heard away from the nest.

Except for winter assemblies in mouse-infested fields, the short-ear is a bird of the marshes, almost invariably nesting within one, using no more than a slight depression in the ground to which is added a minuscule quantity of grass and feathers as lining. But nests on top of low bushes and within burrows in banks are known. The female is burdened with the incubation, brooding and feeding of the young, all of which are assured daily rations by the male.

Pay them a visit at this time and you'll be greeted by a wounded-bird act, including the feigned capture of a victim, equalling the performance staged by the long-ear. The

short-ear also guards its territory as zealously as any kingbird, driving away marsh hawks, crows and other birds of comparable size and threat.

Short-ears enjoy their siesta sometimes in a thick evergreen, sometimes in a clump of grass in a marsh, meadow, slough or plain, where they will remain until almost stepped upon. Irrigated land and alders along lakeshores will also attract them, as will (shades of Shakespeare) cemeteries.

It was while working on other parts of this book that my younger son directed me to a winter group of four. They had pre-empted a small but fairly thick evergreen, part of a row planted on the median of the access road to a park. The cars, which passed quite regularly and within six metres of their roost, had no effect on the birds. I and at least two other photographers took pictures as close as telescopic lens will allow, the birds evincing no interest. In fact, all my chirping and squeaking failed to get the dominant bird to look directly at me. The four looked like drowsy, contented kittens.

A major puzzle in the bird's life history is the choice of *flammeus* as its scientific name. This is Latin for flaming, but since the bird has no feathering of reddish tint, Pontoppidan, who named the bird, must have been examining his specimen through rose-colored glasses.

Saw-whet Owl *(Aegolius acadicus)*

Summers from a line joining the southernmost point of Alaska, the top of Lake Winnipeg and the Gaspé Peninsula south to southern Mexico; but absent from southeastern United States (the states touching the Gulf of Mexico and the Atlantic states south of Virginia). Winters throughout all except the northernmost part of its breeding range and all the United States.

One of the most engaging occupants my house has ever known was a diminutive saw-whet owl, part of the extra-curricular biology studies of my older son. Cute, fearless, unyielding and uncowed were adjectives describing it better than the feather-by-feather accounts in ornithologies. It ceased to be a member of the household soon after the distaff side discovered that house mice introduced into its cage had a disconcerting habit of slipping through the bars to take refuge in some innermost recess of the building. The sequel was a mouse trap in every finger-catching cranny.

Saw-whets are most easily found in late fall and early winter, when they congregate in some favored locality. For many years Toronto's islands stood high in the owls' esteem, but latterly their attention has switched to Kingston, 300 kilometres to the east. There, or to be more precise, at Prince Edward point, banders now have their hands and nets full each October. One of the more than 200 saw-whets banded there in 1977 came from Chestertown, Maryland.

Their concentration at certain points on the north shore of Lake Ontario suggests their migration path in fall follows that of hawks, westward at least to the end of Lake Ontario, where they find a shorter water crossing.

One way to locate a saw-whet is to monotonously thread thickets until one is spotted. I speeded up the process one March by using Boy Scout tactics. Alerted to the presence of one in a nearby valley, I viewed its shelter, a large thicket of willow, with the dismay of a mother about to tidy the room of a young son. Then I brightened. Large footprints, disfiguring a fresh snowfall, marked the path of the bird's finder. I began to trace them, slowly weaving through the slender, naked canes until I was brought to a sudden halt, transfixed by two unblinking orbs of yellow on level with, and an arm's length from my own. The owl was obviously questioning the unseemly violation of its sanctuary.

Deer hunters will be more successful in finding this owl than will many birders. Maintaining lonely vigil on some stand in leafless November, their eyes, in constant quest of tangible evidence of life, will pick up the owl's motionless form. In fact, it was the sound of a falling pellet that attracted one hunter to his strigiform companion.

Not only is the saw-whet easily overlooked when at rest, it is just as easily passed off as something else when in flight. Then it appears as a heavily burdened neckless woodpecker, flying with laboring, undulating flight. It can also bear an uncanny resemblance to a flying woodcock.

Certain of its summer retreats differ little from the habitat of that aberrant shorebird. Rubber footwear is required when penetrating the cedar and tamarack bogs and swamps that claim it for the warmer half of the year, where it will roost by day in a hole or close to the trunk of one of the thickest evergreens in its preserve. In winter it will seek the shelter of barns and similar buildings, capitalizing on the mice that have also taken abode there for the food to be found in the interior.

Of its several calls, its most common one is the origin of its odd name. It is a sound that was once heard frequently about the house, when its master or the man-of-all-work applied file to a dull saw, shredding nerve ends until they resembled an old shaving brush. The "saw-sharpening season" begins in late winter, starts to fall off in spring and concludes in June.

A second call, more pleasing to the ears of humans and female saw-whets alike, is the male's courtship song. Like the boreal's, it sounds like falling water, but is delivered so rapidly and interminably as to be compared to a drizzle rather than a drip. To some, it is a metallic *ping* or *tang*; to others, it is more like the strident *zing-g-g* of a grasshopper. Still others claim it is a soft sound, a rapid repetition of the syllable *too* or *whoop*, comparable to the deliberately spaced *poo* of the European Tengmalm's owl. The industrious banders at Kingston, referred to previously, discovered another note, an evenly spaced clicking sound coming from the syrinx only. The sound could be emitted by an owl with a billful of mouse.

An abandoned flicker's abode is preferred for nesting and, in its absence, a tree cavity or even a fissure in rocks. No lining other than its own dropped feathers will be used. In emergency it will use the nests of small birds or the dreys of squirrels, and is still one

more species affected by the removal of elms that have succumbed to Dutch elm disease. Tapping a tree containing a likely hole may bring a bird to the opening, when a mild retaliation may ensue. If the bird in view is a fledgling, you are in for a surprise. Young saw-whets wear a chocolate brown plumage so different to the dress of their parents and for such a lengthy period that they were long considered a separate species called "Kirtland's owl."

The species has also been labelled "tame," "stupid," and "fearless," when, in fact, it is merely uncomprehending. It is so nocturnal and so retiring that its contacts with man have been too infrequent for the owl to regard him as anything but a curiosity. For that reason, the bird can be approached or called up so closely that it can be stroked or even caught by hand.

As it is the smallest of our eastern owls and one of the most nocturnal, it is victimized by other owls abroad at the same time particularly to the indiscriminating taste of the long-ear.

In winter, when mice have tunnelled along limbs heavily coated with snow, look for a spot on the branch that is bare. The saw-whet looks for such spots, too, and patiently waits for a mouse to emerge from the subway. And that is a second way to locate a saw-whet.

Boreal Owl *(Aegolius funereus)*

In North America, found from a little below the tree line from Alaska to central Labrador, south to, but not including, the tip of Vancouver Island, the top of Lake Superior and the bottom of coastal Labrador. In Eurasia, from the tree line south to the cordillera. In North America, winters sporadically south to New England and the northern tier of states in United States.

For a small owl that lives in the far north and is seen by few people, this bird has a lot of names, some of them almost as long as the bird itself. One name is "phillip-pile-tshish," which, to assist in pronunciation, is sometimes abbreviated to "phillip-ile-tschch." Both mean "water-dripping-owl," and originate in the legend of an Indian tribe. The story goes that the largest owl in the world, proud of its great size, tried to match decibels with a roaring waterfall. This impertinence so angered the Great Spirit that the owl woke the next morning to find he had become a diminutive thing and that his voice had been reduced to the sound of softly dripping water. The Eskimos up Alaska way call it "tuk-whe-ling-uk," which translates into "the blind one."

The original English name of the North American race was Richardson's owl, after Sir John Richardson, the 19th century Arctic explorer who, alone or in collaboration with William Swainson, wrote of the fauna of the Canadian arctic. The scientific name of the North American race perpetuates Richardson's name. The English call the Old World form Tengmalm's owl.

Although its "song" may sound like the dripping of water and justify one Indian cognomen, the bird does not deserve the appelation "blind." It is easily caught by hand, not because its eyesight is poor, but because it does not associate danger with the humans it meets so infrequently. Other than being momentarily dazzled when opening its eyes in bright light, it can see very well.

Because its home is that coniferous belt that bands the north, it lives a life uncomplicated by human intervention. Favoring edges where the omnipresent spruce mixes with other kinds of tree growth, it subsists on small rodents and some insects. When these can shelter under snow or become dormant, as the case may be, the owl will wreak havoc among wandering flocks of arboreal finches.

Its emigrations to the south at such times are ordinarily no more than a dribble. One notable irruption occurred in the winter of 1922-23, when it was markedly evident that such birds seemed lost, and so unable to comprehend the food value of the many small winter birds surrounding them that emaciation and death followed. One boreal owl was frequent visitor to a feeding station, its companions juncos and tree sparrows, birds it was not familiar with in its northern home. In the midst of such bounty the owl starved while the sparrows and juncos, just as ignorant of the owl, were unperturbed even when the owl was quite near.

An interesting revelation during a minor influx to southern Ontario in February, 1978, was the number of flying squirrels found in the stomachs of specimens. The northern limit of the range of the boreal owl and the northern flying squirrel is almost identical, yet the mammal has been accorded small place in a list of the bird's food items. Also interesting was the appearance at the same time of an abnormal number of redpolls, featured on the owl's winter menu in the north. An enterprising student will find these relationships worth further study and may have more opportunities in the future than have been presented in the past. The influxes of 1954-5, 1962-3 and 1968-9 were almost equalled in the three winters ending in 1977-8.

The boreal owl is quite nocturnal during its rare visits to the south, the reverse of its nature in summer when, perforce, it must end its daytime siesta when the sky is still quite bright. It is so averse to southern sunshine that, in addition to roosting in thick trees by day, it will enter barns and other outbuildings and was once found in a haystack. In the north it often shelters in deserted igloos. It also makes use of holes and cavities for nesting. The abandoned home of a pileated woodpecker is favored over that of a flicker as the latter's is a tight fit.

The soft, liquid notes that sound like drops of water falling into a container from a height constitute its song. The series of up to ten are high-pitched and far-carrying and close to being a monotone. They are given by the male while circling either the nest site or the tree in which his mate is perched. The bell-like notes sound like *ting, ting, ting,* although an annoyed male will drop all pretence of a loving disposition and render them in a harsh, grating tone.

The tinkling quality seems to be lacking in Old World birds, whose call is written as *poo, poo, poo*, in a more rapid, shorter series, with some variation in time. The difference recalls the investigation into the alder flycatcher, strongly suspected of being two species because of two totally dissimilar songs attributed to it. The well-founded suspicion produced the distinct willow flycatcher. Students seeking another avenue of research might investigate the two races of the boreal owl. They may also prove to be as genetically distinct as the alder and willow flycatchers.

Food Summaries

As a matter of expediency, the food of the twenty-seven species figured in this book has been tabulated in one section rather than being included in narrative form under each species. The percentages shown are a composite resulting from studying similar breakdowns published elsewhere. The groups are arranged in order of importance or popularity.

The vertebrates are shown by orders, the invertebrates by classes, while the smallest and largest species or group of species are given in parentheses. "T" indicates a trace or, at most, less than 1%.

Turkey Vulture
100 Carrion
  T Offal
  T Excrement (pigs' – sealions')
  T Insects (grasshoppers)
  T Snakes
  T Waders, young and eggs
     (ibises – herons)
  T Rodents (mice)
  T Artiodactyls (young pigs)
  T Vegetable (rotting fruits –
     rotting vegetables)
  T Poultry
     (young and weak chickens)

Osprey
100 Fishes up to 2 kg.:
     Sturgeon
     Herrings (alewives – salmon)
     Eels
     Minnows (suckers – carp)
     Catfishes
       (bullheads – sea catfish)
     Pike
     Burbot (tomcod – flounders)
     Perch
       (sunfish – bass in hatcheries)
  T Snails (sea snails)
  T Crustaceans
  T Insects (beetles)
  T Amphibians
  T Turtles
  T Snakes
     (water snakes – sea snakes)
  T Birds:
     Petrels
       (storm petrels, wounded?)
     Ducks (young mallards)

Shorebirds (sandpipers)
Perchers (jackdaws)
  T Mammals
  T Carrion

Bald Eagle
(A large part is
definitely carrion)
 76 Fishes:
     Herrings (alewives – salmon)
     Minnows (chub – carp)
     Catfishes
       (bullheads – lake catfish)
     Pike (sand pike – blue pike)
     Perches
       (yellow perch – black bass)
  9 Game Birds:
     Ducks
       (lesser scaup – Canada goose)
     Grouse
       (ptarmigan – wild turkey)
  8 Mammals:
     Carnivores
       (weasel – gray fox)
     Rodents
       (squirrel – porcupine)
     Rabbits (marsh rabbit)
     Artiodactyls
       (young lambs – young fawns)
  5 Miscellaneous:
     Offal
     Carrion
     Crustaceans (crabs)
     Amphibians
     Turtles
     Snakes (lizards – fox snake)
     Non-Game Birds: 212
     Rails (coot)

Shorebirds (tern – murre)
Waders (little blue heron –
   snowy egret)
Cormorants
   (double-crested cormorant)
Grebes (pied-billed – horned)
Perchers
   (savannah sparrow – crow)

Marsh Hawk
 41 Rodents (mouse – cotton rat)
 40 Non-Game Birds:
     Perchers (wren – grackle)
     Woodpeckers (flicker)
     Owls (screech owl)
     Hawks (American kestrel)
     Herons (green heron –
        American bittern)
  5 Other Mammals:
     Insectivores (shrew – mole)
     Rabbits (cottontail)
     Carnivores (young skunk)
  4 Game Birds:
     Rails (clapper rail – coot)
     Ducks
       (green-winged teal and larger)
     Shorebirds
       (sandpipers – plover)
     Grouse (bobwhite –
        ring-necked pheasant)
     Pigeons (mourning dove)
     Poultry (young and
        far-wandering adults)
  4 Amphibians
  3 Snakes (lizards – snakes)
  3 Insects (crickets – locusts)
  T Carrion
  T Offal

  T Crustaceans (crayfish)
  T Fishes
  T Birds' Eggs
     (ground nesters)

Northern Goshawk
 53 Game Birds:
     Grouse (bobwhite –
        ring-necked pheasant)
     Ducks (green-winged teal –
        mallard)
     Pigeons (mourning dove –
        feral pigeon)
     Poultry
     Shorebirds (common snipe)
 30 Mammals:
     Rabbits
       (cottontail – Arctic hare)
     Rodents (lemming –
        woodchuck)
     Insectivores (shrew)
     Carnivores
       (weasel – young lynx)
 17 Non-Game Birds:
     Perchers
       (house sparrow – crow)
     Woodpeckers
       (hairy woodpecker)
     Kingfishers
       (belted kingfisher)
     Gulls (thick-billed murre –
        black-headed gull)
     Owls (up to barred)
     Hawks (American kestrel)
  T Reptiles (lizards – snakes)
  T Insects
     (beetle larvae – locusts)
  T Snails
  T Carrion

Sharp-shinned Hawk

86 Non-Game Birds:
   Perchers (wren – gray jay)
   Shorebirds (sandpipers)
   Woodpeckers
     (downy – pileated)
   Swifts (chimney swift)
   herons
     (black-crowned night)
7 Insects (crickets – locusts)
6 Rodents (mouse – red squirrel)
1 Game Birds:
   Grouse (bobwhite)
   Pigeons (mourning dove –
     domestic pigeon)
   Poultry (half-grown)
T Amphibians
T Snakes (lizards – snakes)
T Other Mammals:
   Insectivores (shrew)
   Bats
   Rabbits (young)

Cooper's Hawk

59 Non-Game Birds:
   Perchers
     (warblers – common grackle)
   Woodpeckers (flicker)
   Kingfishers
     (belted kingfisher)
   Hawks (American kestrel)
   Herons
     (least bittern – little blue)
   Owls (screech owl)
23 Game Birds:
   Shorebirds (common snipe)
   Grouse
     (bobwhite – blue grouse)
   Pigeons
     (mourning dove –
     feral pigeon)
   Poultry
17 Mammals:
   Rabbits
     (cottontail – varying hare)
   Rodents
     (house mouse – Norway rat)
   Carnivores (skunk)
   Opossums
1 *Combined*
   Insects
     (crickets – grasshoppers)
   Fishes (minnows)
   Amphibians
   Snakes (lizards – snakes)

Red-shouldered Hawk

27 Rodents
     (deer mouse – muskrat)
23 Amphibians (frogs – toads)
12 Other Mammals:
   Insectivores (shrew – mole)
   Rabbits (young cottontail)
   Opossums
   Carnivores (skunks)
12 Reptiles:
   Snakes
     (lizards – water snakes)
   Turtles
11 Insects
     (larvae – dragonflies)
6 Non-Game Birds:
   Perchers
     (house sparrow – crow)
   Woodpeckers (flicker)
   Hawks (American kestrel)
   Owls (screech owl)
5 Crustaceans (crayfish)
3 Spiders
1 Game Birds:
   Grouse (bobwhite –
     ring-necked pheasant)
   Pigeons (mourning dove)
   Shorebirds
     (American woodcock)
   Rails (sora)
T Carrion and Offal
T Earthworms
T Snails
T Centipedes
T Fishes (catfish)

Broad-winged Hawk

36 Insects (ants – dragonflies)
21 Rodents
     (meadow vole – Norway rat)
14 Amphibians
     (wood frog – toad)
11 Snakes
     (lizards – small snakes)
8 Other Mammals:
   Insectivores (shrew – mole)
   Rabbits
     (cottontail – varying hare)
   Carnivores (weasel)
5 Non-Game Birds:
   Perchers
     (goldfinch – brown thrasher)
   Woodpeckers (flicker)
3 Earthworms

Red-tailed Hawk

2 Crustaceans (crayfish)
T Centipedes
T Millipedes
T Spiders
T Fishes (minnows)

41 Rodents
     (deer mouse – porcupine)
35 Other Mammals:
   Rabbits
     (cottontail – jack-rabbit)
   Insectivores (shrew – mole)
   Carnivores (weasel – raccoon)
   Bats
8 Reptiles:
   Snakes
     (lizards – rattlesnakes)
   Turtles
   Amphibians (wood frog – toad)
7 Non-Game Birds:
   Perchers (house wren – crow)
   Woodpeckers
   Kingfishers
     (belted kingfisher)
   Hawks
     (red-shouldered, exceptional)
   Owls (screech owl)
6 Game Birds:
   Grouse
     (scaled quail – young turkey)
   Shorebirds (common snipe)
   Pigeons (mourning dove)
   Rails (rails – gallinule)
   Ducks
     (green-winged teal – pintail)
2 Insects
     (crickets – grasshoppers)
1 Fishes:
   Carp, possibly stranded
   Catfish
T Carrion and offal
T Earthworms
T Crustaceans (land crab)
T Centipedes

Rough-legged Buzzard

79 Rodents
     (lemming – prairie dog)
7 Insects
     (crickets – grasshoppers)
6 Other Mammals:
   Insectivores (shrew – mole)
   Rabbits

(cottontail – European hare)
   Carnivores (weasel)
2 Carrion
2 Snakes (lizards – snakes)
2 Non-Game Birds:
   Perchers
     (snow bunting – meadowlark)
   Grebes (pied-billed grebe)
1 Amphibians (toads – frogs)
1 Offal
   Game Birds:
   Grouse (spruce grouse)
   Ducks (ruddy duck,
     probably crippled)
   Crustaceans (crayfish)
   Mussels (shellfish)

Golden Eagle

(much of larger items
may be carrion)
82 Mammals:
   Rabbits
     (cottontail – jack-rabbit)
   Rodents
     (lemming – hoary marmot)
   Carnivores
     (weasel – domestic dog)
   Insectivores (mole)
   Artiodactyls (young pig –
     weak, trapped deer)
   Opossums
8 Game Birds:
   Grouse (bobwhite – turkey)
   Ducks (ducks – geese)
   Shorebirds
     (plovers – curlews)
   Pigeons (band-tailed pigeon)
   Poultry
6 Non-Game Birds:
   Perchers (thrush – magpie)
   Rails (coot)
   Kingfishers
     (belted kingfisher)
   Owls (short-eared owl)
   Hawks
     (goshawk – red-tailed hawk)
   Herons (great blue heron,
     exceptional)
4 Carrion
T Offal
T Insects (grasshoppers)
T Fishes (probably dead)
T Snakes
     (lizards – rattlesnakes)

American Kestrel
59 Insects (ants – dragonflies)
23 Rodents
(deer mouse – chipmunk)
12 Birds:
Perchers (chipping sparrow –
meadowlark)
Grouse
(young ring-necked pheasant)
Poultry (young)
5 Snakes
(lizards – garter snake)
1 Spiders
T Amphibians (frog)
T Other Mammals:
Insectivores (shrew)
Bats (small)

Merlin
64 Non-Game Birds:
Perchers
(kinglets – blue jay)
Woodpeckers (flicker)
Swifts (chimney swift –
black swift)
Petrels (Leach's petrel)
31 Insects
(crickets – dragonflies)
3 Rodents
(meadow vole – squirrels)
1 Game Birds:
Shorebirds (sanderling –
European curlew)
Pigeons (ground dove –
feral pigeon)
Grouse (California quail)
Ducks (green-winged teal)
1 Amphibians (toad)
Snakes (lizards – snakes)
Other Mammals:
Rabbits (cottontail)
Bats (small)

Gyrfalcon
50 Mammals:
Rabbits
(cottontail – Arctic hare)
Carnivores (weasel – mink)
30 Game Birds:
Grouse (ptarmigan –
prairie chicken)
Pigeons (feral pigeon)
Poultry
Ducks (eiders – geese)

20 Non-Game Birds:
Shorebirds
(dunlin – kittiwake)
Perchers
(winter wren – snow bunting)
Owls (short-eared owl)

Peregrine Falcon
73 Non-Game Birds:
Shorebirds (semipalmated
plover – guillemot)
Perchers (goldfinch – crow)
Woodpeckers
Kingfishers
(belted kingfisher)
Grebes (horned grebe)
Cuckoos
(black-billed cuckoo)
Hawks (kestrel – marsh hawk)
Herons (green heron)
Swifts (chimney swift)
Goatsuckers (whip-poor-
will – nighthawk)
Owls
Petrels (dusky petrel –
shearwaters)
13 Insects
(beetles – dragonflies)
11 Game Birds:
Ducks
(green-winged teal – geese)
Grouse (bobwhite –
ring-necked pheasant)
Rails (rails – coots)
Pigeons (mourning dove –
feral pigeon)
Poultry
3 Rodents
(lemming – woodchuck)
T Rabbits
(cottontail – varying hare)

Barn Owl
80 Rodents
(pine mouse – muskrat)
13 Other Mammals:
Insectivores
(shrew – star-nosed mole)
Rabbits (young cottontail –
black-tailed jack-rabbit)
Bats
Carnivores (spotted skunk)
5 Game Birds:
Pigeons (feral pigeon)

Waterfowl (small ducks)
Rails (sora – clapper rail)
Poultry
1 Non-Game Birds:
Perchers (wrens – blue jay)
Woodpeckers (flicker)
Petrels (Leach's petrel)
Herons (green heron)
1 Insects
(crickets – grasshoppers)
T Amphibians (frogs)
T Snakes (lizards – snakes)
T Fishes
(usually trapped in pools)
T Crustaceans (crayfish)

Screech Owl
42 Rodents (grasshopper
mouse – Norway rat)
25 Insects (ants – locusts)
12 Non-Game Birds:
Perchers
(house wren – blue jay)
Woodpeckers
(downy woodpecker)
Owls (screech owl)
Hawks (American kestrel)
8 Crustaceans (crayfish)
5 Amphibians
(treefrog – bullfrog)
3 Fishes:
Minnows (dace – suckers)
Catfish (horned pout)
Perch (sunfish – bass)
2 Other Mammals:
Insectivores (sorex shrews –
short-tailed shrew)
Bats
Rabbits
(cottontail – swamp rabbit)
2 Game Birds:
Grouse (bobwhite –
ring-necked pheasant)
Poultry
Shorebirds (common snipe –
American woodcock)
Pigeons (mourning dove –
feral pigeon)
Ducks
1 Spiders
(spiders – scorpions)
T Snakes (skinks – snakes)
T Turtles (soft-shells)
T Millipedes

T Centipedes
T Snails
T Earthworms
T Fruits
T Berries

Great Horned Owl
50 Mammals:
Rabbits (brush rabbit –
European hare)
Carnivores (weasel – raccoon)
Bats
Opossums
Insectivores (shrew – mole)
27 Game Birds:
Grouse
(bobwhite – wild turkey)
Poultry (hens – turkeys)
Rails
(Virginia rail – king rail)
Ducks (wood duck – swans)
Pigeons (mourning dove –
feral pigeon)
Shorebirds (red phalarope –
common snipe)
10 Rodents
(pocket mouse – nutria)
7 Non-Game Birds:
Perchers (juncos – raven)
Woodpeckers
(sapsucker – flicker)
Kingfishers
(belted kingfisher)
Owls
(screech owl – barred owl)
Grebes (pied-billed grebe)
5 Insects
(crickets – grasshoppers)
1 Combined
Fishes:
Minnows
(dace – common sucker)
Catfish (horned pout)
Perch (yellow perch)
Eels
Garfish
Spiders
(spiders – scorpions)
T Crustaceans (crayfish – crabs)
T Earthworms
T Centipedes
T Amphibians (salamanders –
frogs)
T Snakes (horned toad – black
snake)
T Turtles (soft-shells)

Snowy Owl

76 Rodents
  (lemming – woodchuck)
  Rabbits
  (cottontail – Arctic hare)
20 Non-Game Birds:
  Perchers (longspurs – raven)
  Owls (screech owl –
  long-eared owl)
  Hawks (young peregrine
  falcon – young gyrfalcon)
  Rails (coots)
  Grebes
4 Game Birds:
  Grouse
  (bobwhite – sage grouse)
  Ducks (oldsquaw –
  young emperor goose)
  Shorebirds (plover – curlew)
  Poultry (hens – Guineafowl)
  Pigeons (mourning dove –
  feral pigeon)
T Other Mammals:
  Carnivores (fox, trapped)
  Insectivores (shrew – mole)
T Fishes (beached)
T Insects
T Meat scraps
T Carrion

Hawk Owl

98 Rodents (lemming –
  ground squirrels)
2 Non-Game Birds:
  Perchers
  (pine siskin – crossbills)
T Other Mammals:
  Rabbits
  (cottontail – varying hare)
  Carnivores (weasel)
  Insectivores (shrew)
T Game Birds:
  Grouse (rock ptarmigan –
  sharp-tailed grouse)
T Insects (grasshoppers)

Barred Owl

49 Rodents (red-backed mouse –
  fox squirrel)
16 Insects
  (crickets – grasshoppers)
10 Amphibians
  (salamanders – frogs)

9 Other Mammals:
  Rabbits (cottontail –
  young varying hare)
  Insectivores (shrew – mole)
  Bats
  Carnivores (weasel – mink)
  Opossums
7 Non-Game Birds:
  Perchers (juncos – crow)
  Woodpeckers
  (downy woodpecker –
  flicker)
  Kingfishers
  (belted kingfisher)
  Owls
  (screech owl – barn owl)
  Rails (purple gallinule)
5 Crustaceans (crayfish)
3 Game Birds:
  Grouse
  (bobwhite – ruffed grouse)
  Poultry (young)
  Pigeons (mourning dove –
  feral pigeon)
  Ducks (young ducks)
1 *Combined*
  Reptiles:
  Snakes (lizards – snakes)
  Turtles
  (box tortoise – terrapin)
  Fishes:
  Minnows (chub – carp)
  Catfish
  Perch (yellow perch – bream)
  Eels
  Spiders (spiders – scorpions)
T Molluscs (snails – slugs)
T Crustaceans
  (crayfish – fiddler crab)

Great Gray Owl

74 Rodents
  (meadow vole – red
  squirrel)
19 Other Mammals:
  Rabbits
  (cottontail – varying hare)
  Insectivores (shrew)
7 Non-Game Birds:
  Perchers
  (common redpoll – crow)
T Game Birds:
  Grouse
  (ptarmigan – ruffed grouse)
  Poultry

Long-eared Owl

82 Rodents (prairie meadow
  vole – squirrels)
17 Non-Game Birds:
  Perchers
  (kinglets – common jay)
  Owls (screech owl)
1 Other Mammals:
  Insectivores (shrew – mole)
  Bats (myotis bats)
  Rabbits (cottontail)
T Snakes (small)
T Amphibians (frogs)
T Fishes
T Insects
  (beetles – cockchafers)

Short-eared Owl

81 Rodents
  (pine mouse – muskrat)
15 Non-Game Birds:
  Perchers
  (kinglets – grackles)
  Woodpeckers
  (sapsuckers – flickers)
  Shorebirds (common tern)
4 Insects
  (cutworms – grasshoppers)
T Other Mammals:
  Rabbits (cottontail)
  Bats
  Insectivores (shrew – mole)
T Game Birds:
  Grouse (quail – ring-necked
  pheasant)
  Rails (black rail – sora)
  Shorebirds (common snipe)

Saw-whet Owl

86 Rodents (red-backed mouse –
  flying squirrel)
11 Non-Game Birds:
  Perchers
  (warblers – song sparrow)
  Pigeons (feral pigeon)
3 Insects
T Other Mammals:
  Rabbits
  (cottontail – varying hare)
  Insectivores (shrew – mole)
  Bats
  Carnivores (least weasel)
T Amphibians (frogs)
T Carrion

Boreal Owl

59 Rodents
  (lemming – flying squirrel)
33 Other Mammals:
  Insectivores (shrew – mole)
  Bats
8 Non-Game Birds:
  Perchers (redpoll)
T Insects
  (crickets – grasshoppers)
T Amphibians
  (salamanders – frogs)
T Snakes (lizards – snakes)

Falconry

When man, who may not have resembled the present-day specimen, descended from the trees to forage on the ground in Africa, the supposed place of his emergence, his taste buds were very similar to those of the bears whose hides he was to eventually covet in perhaps, another land. Fruits and nuts he already knew, having plucked them when he shared their arboreal quarters. Now, on the ground, he sampled and enjoyed more terrestrial fare: Tubers, berries, large insects, small rodents and even carrion, for he had no way of obtaining large mammals in a fresh state.

During his arboreal existence, he had pelted earth-bound enemies with many a ripe fruit or hard nut and may have even hurled a broken branch at some snarling foe, in the same manner as Jane Goodall's chimps. Now his arsenal included stones picked from the ground which he learned to throw with the unerring precision of a major league baseball player. Larger rocks were no doubt heaved in two-handed fashion, an event missing from modern Olympiads. Fallen branches were both swung and tossed with energy. But, one day, a nicely weighted branch became a club. Thenceforth, no household was complete without a cudgel.

Perhaps at about the same time, one hunter (he may also have been the hunted) threw a branch as one throws a stone, scored a bull's-eye, then reasoned that the attachment of one of his sharp, skinning stones might make the weapon more effective. And so the spear was born.

My imaginary delving into the development of weapons for both defence and for hunting stops there. Obviously, at some further time, some enterprising forerunner of ours found that a piece of sinew tied to each end of a stiff, yet flexible branch would propel a straight, polished, tipped shaft faster, farther and more accurately than his arm could hurl a spear. Imagination does produce a scenario where the inventor of the bow-and-arrow is surrounded by admirers of both sexes. During his immodest reception of much adulation, he no doubt pointed to one comely member of the opposite sex and stated: "Me Tarzan. You cook." Women's Lib is only now recovering from the setback.

The bow-and-arrow (bownarrer to uncouth contemporaries of an early age; bownarrow to the intelligentsia) was, in more ways than one, a hit. It produced food, and with a slight margin of safety. There was less effort expended than in stampeding herds of ungulates over cliffs or digging pits to entrap them. Except for a few refinements and some tangent weapons, such as the bolero and the boomerang, the bow-and-arrow was for centuries the ultimate weapon for self defence and the procurement of food.

In those days, everyone, of course, was an outdoors enthusiast. Living on intimate terms with wildlife, prehistoric man had greater knowledge of the lives and habits of animals than does the well-educated high-rise man of today. He was also aware that the hawks, in which he had no interest table-wise, were accomplished hunters; and, further, that they took the same small game, such as rabbits, grouse, quail and ducks he himself found so tasty. Thus, there was born in a very obscure time of history, the idea of training a hawk as a surrogate killer. The person conceiving the thought must have been an Oriental, as the oldest records of falconry date back 4,000 years into the dim history of China and the Far East. Perhaps the Pekin Man had a hand in it!

Hunting with hawks was superior to using the bow-and-arrow because man no longer needed stealth and subterfuge in his approach to quarry but could send his emissary instead. Undoubtedly, many hawks used venatically were lost; but so, too, were arrows. It is reasonable to assume that falconry did not replace hunting with the bow. It did make certain game, quite often delicacies, more accessible.

Falconry was confined to the Far East for many, many years. Not until 1700 B.C. do we find evidence of it in the Middle East, where there has been unearthed bas-reliefs showing men carrying hawks on their wrists. Falconry in some of those countries, Arabia, Syria and Persia especially, is still something more than mere sport. Notwithstanding its start in the Far East, falconry did not seem to be practised in Japan until 600 B.C.

Pliny the Elder and Aristotle, two erstwhile feature editors who neglected few popular topics, wrote of falconry as it was practised in Greece during the fourth to second centuries before Christ. It did not, however, seem to appeal to the ancient Greeks who lived in a land that abounded in hawks at that time; nor was it popular with the later Romans, who dismissed it and the barbarians who practised it with equal contempt.

Central Europeans were practising it either for hunting or amusement by the third or fourth century A.D., and in the sixth, the Lombards carried it with them into northern Italy. There is some evidence of it in Britain as early as the sixth if not even the fifth century, but it was not formally introduced there until 860 A.D., by which time it had become established in western Europe.

From the 13th to 17th centuries, falconry flourished in Britain and western Europe, receiving a large impulse in the 16th, when crusaders returned from their mission bringing with them knowledge of the art acquired from practitioners in the lands where they warred. The sight of a hawk perched on a fist became commonplace, even in church!

Whatever its use, to obtain provender or merely for sport, falconry declined with the introduction of firearms. Fowling pieces offered greater guarantee of food for the larder than did the best-trained falcon. Its appeal as a sport began to wane, too, as the large estates were subdivided, fenced and removed from the ken of the falconer and his bird. Falconry came to a halt during the English Civil War but was revived by enthusiasts from time to time, with considerable interest displayed in recent years.

The quaint terms still used in falconry attest to its popularity in mediaeval England. The origin of some is lost, but many were derived from the French, as France served as the springboard for its leap into England.

A falconer is one who flies hawks, the term being, perhaps, all-embracing. An *Austringer* or *Ostringer* is one who flies a short-winged accipiter as opposed to a long-winged falcon. It is derived from the Latin *astor*, which gave rise to *astur*, the one-time generic name of the goshawk, and means starry-eyed. Hunting hawks are normally kept in a *hawk-house*, being removed to the *mews* to moult. A sleeping hawk goes *to jowke* or *to jouk*. Hawks do not defecate but *mute* (falcons) or *slice* (accipiters), although the droppings of either are *mutes*.

A short-winged hawk ready to be flown at quarry is *in yarak*. The list is endless, sometimes devious in etymology, yet always interesting.

Interesting, too, are the terms given a hawk in its progress through life.

Falconers divide the diurnal raptors into two kinds, remarkably consistent with the view of modern taxonomists. The first division includes only the falcons, which are called *long-winged hawks*, and which the French call the *ramiers* or rowers, because of their wing-action in flight. They are trained to come to the lure. In falconry, only the female peregrine is called a falcon. The short-winged hawks, or *voiliers* (sailors), include all members of the family *Accipitridae*, and are trained to come to the fist. E. M. Michell proposed eagles as a third class on the grounds that they were neither hawks nor falcons, but the distinction is not tenable as certain so-called eagles are merely large buteonine hawks or buzzards.

The bird begins, of course, as an egg. On hatching, it is said to be *disclosed*, at which time it is a nestling or *eyass*, from the French *niais* or nest. When able to move about on its feet it is a *ramager*. Nest exercises are followed by the bird moving out of the nest and hopping about nearby branches, making it a *brancher*. Up to this time the bird will be *unsummed*, but now, fully feathered, it will be *summed*. Most species will be a reddish brown before assuming adult plumage, and will be called a *soar* or *sore* hawk, from the French *sor*, Latin *saurus*, both meaning reddish brown. When migration time begins the young bird becomes a *passager* or *passage* hawk. At the end of the first calendar year after hatching, it is given the term *antennaire*, from the French *antan*, meaning yesteryear, and becomes a *Lent* hawk or *lentiner* (also *lantiner*) the first Lent following.

If the hawk is caught after leaving the nest but before migrating, it is a *gentle* or *slight* hawk. After moulting, a wild hawk is known as a *haggard*, while one in the same condition in captivity is said to be *intermewed*. In either event, the bird will now have the feathering of an adult.

The various hawks and falcons respond differently to training and hunting, some providing a greater thrill than others. These reasons, plus the relative scarcity, resulted in virtual royal decrees over what class of people were entitled to what kind of hawk. The kinds used and the classes to which they were assigned, follows:

1. Eagle – Emperor. Carried for prestige and then chiefly on parades. The eagle's use in falconry was restricted to wolf hunting. It is a difficult bird to train and handle, and is always potentially dangerous. The Emperor's hawk-house would, of course, be well filled and would contain all kinds.

2. Gyrfalcon – Kings and queens. Flown to herons, cranes, kites, buzzards and other large broad-winged hawks, the birds taking no interest in the kill as food. Males show little response, perhaps because the defence of the nest against hereditary enemies such as eagles falls to the larger female.

3. Peregine falcon, female – Princes, dukes, earls and other nobility. The most popular bird in North America and western Europe. The peregine is flown to game birds such as grouse and ducks.

4. Peregrine falcon, male (tiercel, i.e., one-third smaller than a female) – Barons.

5. Saker falcon – Knight. The saker is a desert falcon of the Middle East, where it is preferred to the peregrine.

6. Lanner falcon – Squire. A desert falcon of Africa, where it is also preferred to the peregrine. History does not record how two relatively poor individuals,

the knight and the squire, were able to procure these exotic birds.

7. Merlin – Lady. Flown to skylarks in the past, now to any kind of similarly sized bird that seeks escape through flight.

8. Hobby – Young man. An Old World species addicted to catching large insects. No doubt used by the young person to train him to falconry.

9. Goshawk, female – Yeoman. Flown to a wide range of feathered game as well as rabbits and hares. They were known as kitchen hawks because they assured a full larder. Goshawks are highly prized from the Near East and eastward, where the peregrine is accorded scant attention.

10. Goshawk, male – Poor man.

11. Sparrow hawk, female – Priest. This in an Old World accipiter, replaced in North America by the sharp-shinned hawk. The sparrow hawk is used to capture small birds up to quail in size. The sharp-shin has been trained for the same purpose as has the larger North American Cooper's hawk. The quarry of the latter would be correspondingly larger.

12. Sparrow hawk, male – Holy Water clerk, a category which defies understanding in today's time.

13. Kestrel – Knave, serf, servant or *villein*. Both Old World and North American kestrels are of little use in falconry. Some birds will attack starlings and even mourning doves, but are not sufficiently aggressive to be used for sport.

Royalty or near-royalty was a prerequisite to falconry in the past, as the training and care of the hawks is a full-time job. Any modern man aspiring to the title of falconer must be both wealthy and unemployed. Royalty, of course, had little if anything to do with the training or care of the birds, tasks undertaken by falconers on the royal "payroll." Adding to them the other vassals connected with the sport gave the king a standing army in itself. The Kubla Khan called on 10,000 beaters when afield to be sure his birds did not strike out. Only a few of his 500 birds, 200 of which were gyrs, would be flown each day.

Some later crowned heads were enthusiasts, although not to the extent of calling on all castle hands at the time of a field expedition. The list reads like a Who's Who of royalty: Catherine II of Russia; Louis XI and Francis I of France; Henry of Navarre; Frederick II of Prussia; and even Pope Leo X took time off from papal chores to relax with his hawks. Closer to home were James IV of Scotland and a long list of British kings starting with Henry the Fowler through Ethelbert the Ready, Harold, Edward III, Henry VI, Henry VIII, Elizabeth I and the aforementioned James, who became the first of that name to head England. Charles II elevated the Duke of St. Albans to the title of Hereditary Grand Falconer of England, an office which, following the adherence of the English to ritual, still exists. Some of the royal personages laid down elaborate laws which were partly responsible for the caste system of ownership. The theft of a trained hawk was a serious misdemeanor; nor could one take eggs or a wild hawk with impunity. The value placed on the birds was very high. Twelve gyrfalcons redeemed the ransom of a kidnapped prince. And all the while St. Bavo of Valkenswaard still looks down benignly from his exalted position of Patron Saint of Falconry.

Over the course of many centuries the practicality of falconry was lost until it was reduced to a purely sporting venture. The practical side of it made some recovery during the past couple of wars, when trained falcons struck down hostile carrier pigeons. They have also been used, with limited success, to rid airports of unwanted gulls and other birds congregating on the runways. A prairie falcon and a golden eagle were "hired" by Toronto International Airport to reduce birds and European hares respectively, but the experiment was not altogether successful as both birds decided to ply their trade elsewhere.

There are two sides to falconry that must be reiterated time and time again. Only the wealthy and therefore persons with ample time and money can indulge in the hobby and nests, eggs, young and adults of certain endangered species must be inviolate, with penalties for lawlessness much more severe than when knighthood was blooming.

Nor can falconry be pursued by the ignorant. A falconer must be able to identify and be familiar with the habits of all hawks, whether the species is used in falconry or not. In the following example the falconer knew his birds well enough but, through the hobby, met a person quite ignorant of feathered life. The falconer was chagrined when his female goshawk brought down a gallinule some distance from the point of cast-off. As he later discovered, the gallinule, hotly pursued by the hawk, dropped to the ground in front of the door of a farmhouse just as the door was opened. The gallinule immediately scurried into the parlor and took refuge in a collection of indoor greenery. In typical goshawk fashion, the short-winged hawk followed on foot. When the austringer arrived he was informed that there was "an eagle in the house eating our aspidistra!"

The Dangerous Pesticides

The diminishing populations of a number of predatory birds was noticed as far back as the late forties. The peregrine falcon, one of the four diurnal raptors included, received the greatest amount of investigation, at least initially; but research was also conducted into the lives of the bald eagle, osprey and merlin, the other three hawk species; and the brown pelican.

Ultimately, a pesticide, DDT, was named the culprit, but investigators later admitted that any one of certain other pesticides, namely, aldrin, dieldrin, heptachlor and chlordane, as well as mercury, could have been contributing agents, either alone or in combination with others. It was also admitted that loss of habitat, either directly or through disturbance by man, could have played some part.

The following is a condensation of the findings of various scientists, scientific bodies and conventions held to determine the specific reason for the decline in numbers.

Every war the world has known had introduced some new technologies and World War II was far from an exception. Not only were new weapons devised, but methods were developed to protect or feed the populace on both sides of the battle lines. Chemists and physicists in particular were very busy and very productive, for warfare was fast approaching the Buck Rogers style of annihilation through guided missiles, lethal rays and deadly poisons. One of the outcomes was a chlorinated hydrocarbon called DDT, compounded in 1874 by O. Zeidler, a German chemist. It was first used on a large scale during World War II to protect American army personnel from insect-borne diseases. Commercially, it began life in 1947.

Labelled as a pesticide which would put an end to man's discomfort from insect pests and better the quality and quantity of his fruit and grain crops, DDT was sprayed widely and indiscriminately. Its deadly effect on some insects was almost instantaneous but not very selective, as it killed pestivorous and predatory insects alike. Some it spared entirely; others it killed only originally, becoming ineffective as they later developed immunity. But man, nevertheless, congratulated himself on having won one of the most costly wars ever waged.

In 1955, some ten years after the acceptance of this boon to mankind, the British Nature Conservancy's census of the population of the British form of the peregrine falcon revealed that the numbers of the bird had noticeably declined, the second time since its population had been deliberately reduced during World War II. During those hostilities, the carrier pigeons used extensively were subject to attack by peregrines, requiring the armed forces to deliberately shoot the birds. By the time peace was declared, the pigeons were getting through unscathed, but the falcon was almost extirpated. But in the decade following, the peregrine had returned to two-thirds its prewar figure. Now the population was falling again. What had reversed the trend?

Coincidentally, a similar decline was noted in the population of the race *(anatum)* of the peregrine falcon inhabiting eastern North America. Compounding the mystery or, even perhaps, leading to its solution, similar trends were very evident in the eastern North American populations of the bald eagle and osprey. A parallel downtrend in the merlin was not immediately noticed, as that species is not as conspicuous as are the osprey and eagle, nor does it rival the peregrine as an object of viewing. The brown pelican, a fish-eating seabird, also went into a decline.

Studies of eagles and ospreys showed them to be nesting as before (except, of course, that the number of nests was fewer) but the eggs did not seem to be hatching. It must be remembered that it is much more difficult to monitor the nest life of either of these species than that of a bird like a robin.

The unsuccessful hatching of eagle and osprey eggs was largely dismissed, regretfully, as the inevitable result of inadvertent interference by a burgeoning human population in conjunction with the loss of habitat as man moved into areas previously claimed by those two raptors. Man, however, was encroaching little, if any, on the habitat of the peregrine. How then to account for the declining population of five avian predators, each at the apex of its pertinent food chain?

In 1962, Rachel Carson's *Silent Spring* brought to the attention of readers interested in the world of nature the massive kill-off perpetrated by the now widely used chemical pesticides. Their deadly properties were affecting life far beyond the pests they were intended for. This motivated Derek A. Ratcliffe, a member of the British Nature Conservancy, to try to determine if the growing use of such chemical destroyers was the agent behind the loss of British peregrines.

His studies were greatly assisted through a new research tool, gas chromatography, whereby animal tissue could be analyzed for its chemical composition in most minute parts. Ratcliffe and his associates found the British peregrines contained more DDT and its metabolite residues than did any other British bird. If this were the culprit, why – and how?

Answers to these questions were not immediately forthcoming, but a reply to the question "where?" was received almost at once. Britain, of course, was one of the "wheres," but so was almost all of Europe except a puzzling isolated area in Spain and a spottiness equally puzzling in North America. There, in 1969, the peregrine had become virtually absent from the east, was almost missing in the western United States, but was carrying on business as usual in Alaska, the Canadian arctic and throughout the coast of British Columbia. Unfortunately, Siberia, Australia and Canada's northwest, some of the best peregrine territories, were not investigated.

It seemed quite obvious that DDT had something, if not everything to do with the diminished population. The fly in the ointment (a fly missed in DDT spraying) was that the eggs of birds in some parts of Canada carried twice as much DDT as birds from other parts, yet these birds were otherwise living and reproducing normally, an anomalous situation defying ready solution.

Ornithologists were now finding what was going awry in the breeding of ospreys and eagles. Their customary rituals of courting, mating, nest-building (or repairing) and egg-laying were going on as before. But the shells of the eggs they were laying were found to be thin (and in the passing of time they were to become thinner and in a few instances, absent altogether) so that the weight of the incubating bird was sufficient to crack or even crush the calcareous wall and thus end the life of the embyro.

Ornithological minds reached positive conclusions in 1969, when kestrels, treated with DDE which, with DDD, is a metabolite or residue of DDT, produced thin-shelled eggs. Subsequently, the eggs of peregrines collected about that time were found to have shells thinner than those gathered prior to 1940. In addition, as a side issue in the investigations into the declining population of the California condor, a similar thinning of the shell was found in the eggs of the related turkey vulture.

Since the spray DDT was used to kill insects, an item missing from the food of the five birds under surveillance, how would it enter their system? A review of their habits and diet showed DDT was ingested along with their prey, the birds and fish that had retained quantities of the poison.

The two falcons, the peregrine and merlin, would capture and eat birds that had themselves eaten insects which had been sprayed with DDT. Ospreys, eagles and pelicans received their doses by way of fish which either absorbed the compound directly from the water or from eating organisms living in that environment, the poison having reached lakes and streams by way of the normal runoff.

Had the poison been one of the older types, the birds may have suffered no other ill effects than nausea or diarrhoea, in the process of which the poison would have been eliminated. But DDT carries an insidious feature. It does not deteriorate as do other chemical or organic compounds. The latter, in a comparatively short time, break down into their original components and return to earth, air or water, as the case may be. DDT, and its metalites, DDE and DDD, continue much as the atomic components in nuclear fission. Plutonium 239, for example, takes 24,360 years to lose just half its radioactivity. The amount of DDT reaching fish or small birds was doing them no harm, as their lifetime is short enough that the compound could not build up to a lethal quantity. But the life of the larger raptors is much longer, and each bird or fish ingested meant more poison was introduced into the system, poison that was not flushed out or eliminated as would have been the case with earlier pesticides. This accumulation and retention was not killing the birds themselves but was affecting their reproductive systems in such a way that the DDE metabolite was interfering with the calcium production at a time it was needed to form a properly shelled egg.

As stated at the beginning, perhaps more than one factor was involved, including any number of the new poisons as well as interference in, or loss of habitat. The latter seems to be the chief factor behind the decline in numbers of the California condor, but poisons are also suspected. Thalium sulfate and strychnine have been used to eliminate ground squirrels and the new compound 1080 used to do away with coyotes. Condors could ingest these poisons when feeding on the carcass of the poisoned mammal.

The use of DDT has been banned now for some years, although it is still extensively employed in South and Central America. One result of its discontinuance has been the reversal of trend in the nesting of bald eagles about Chesapeake Bay, long a stronghold for that species in contiguous United States. There, successful nestings now outnumber failures, and it is hoped that the osprey and brown pelican will follow, although newer poisons pose newer threats. Of these, PCBs, or polychlorinated biphenyls, are currently contaminating water (and air, in some places) to an alarming degree, while breeding failures of the golden eagle in Scotland have been attributed to dieldrin. Like PCBs, PCTs (polychlorinated terphenyls) are persistent in the environment. Highly toxic, they have been found in the fatty tissues of Great Lakes herring gulls and could ultimately reach birds of prey such as the osprey and bald eagle. Still another halogenated hydrocarbon, labelled mirex, has resulted in the banning of commercial fishing in New England rivers and coastal waters and sports fishing in Lake Ontario.

PCBs, used more extensively in manufacturing than as a pesticide, reach the environment as industrial wastes. They affect the estrogen level rather than the production of calcium, but the result is the same – fewer birds. The following is a recent example of how carefully a pesticide must be chosen. An organophosphorous insecticide called azodrin was used in Israel to control a species of vole which thrives on alfalfa. Large numbers of small insectivorous and granivorous birds were killed in the process, while hawks and owls were affected in proportion.

The bald eagle, osprey and brown pelican did not completely disappear from their eastern breeding regions. But their numbers were so reduced and their nests so widely scattered as a result that extirpation was but a few years away. However, there has been no evidence of the peregrine falcon nesting in eastern North America south of the Artic since 1962. The subspecies *Falco peregrinus anatum*, once known as the duck hawk, is thought to be close to, if not fully extinct.

With its revival an impossibility, a different tactic was considered: the introduction of another race into the range of *anatum* with the pious hope that it would adapt to, and survive in somewhat different conditions, and in addition, would migrate in normal fashion, to return the following spring to the land of its adoption.

In 1970, Dr. Tom J. Cade, professor of ornithology at Cornell University, began a study of propagating peregrine falcons in captivity, culminating with the successful breeding of peregrines three years later. The propagation involves study of individual birds or pairs, each requiring a different approach to the reproductive goal. Artificial insemination is a frequent practice, as is also artificial incubation where a female is disinclined to do the job herself.

Some young have been introduced into the nests of wild peregrines, others to wild prairie falcons. Still others have been introduced, a week before fledging, to what is termed a hacking station. The young birds are hand-fed there but are gradually weaned until hunger forces them into seeking their own food. Such releases, in eight states, have seen known losses of only one bird in three or four and speaks well for the attempt to fill the void occasioned by the loss of the subspecies *anatum*. Foster parents have been utilized in another four states, so that, all told, reintroduction or augmentation of the peregrine falcon has been conducted in California, Colorado, Idaho, Maryland, Massachusetts, New Hampshire, New Jersey, New Mexico, New York, Pennsylvania, Vermont and Wisconsin.

A similar program was begun in Canada under the direction of Richard Fyfe and J. A. Keith, of the Canadian Wildlife Service. Releases were begun in 1976 in the provinces of Alberta, Ontario and Quebec. The success of this venture can be measured in the history of one bird. It was hatched in an incubator in Alberta, flown to and hacked in Quebec and caught during the migration period at Hawk Cliff, near St. Thomas, Ontario, one of the spots a migrating peregrine raised or nesting in eastern Canada would have passed.

Cade's birds are of the subspecies *tundriensis*, the Artic form, but also include some hybrids. The Canadian program used the western subspecies *pealei*. Both programs, however, were fraught with disheartening mishaps and failures, making each successful introduction a *cause célèbre* of increasing intensity. However, when at least twenty birds were seen in Ontario (Toronto and Point Pelee) in October, 1979, the success of the program seems assured

This program parallels the propagation and release of the almost-extinct whooping crane, its relatively numerous cousin, the sandhill crane, being the unwitting foster parent. To a lesser degree, it also parallels the several programs conducted in Australia, where species or subspecies, as the case may be, have been transferred from an island where the form is still well established to another where the species, subspecies or similar species has been eradicated.

None of these drastic measures would have been necessary had man realized, long ago, that, to control environment and prevent further extermination of species, he must first control and even reduce the human population.

Bibliography

A.O.U. Committee. 1957. *Check-List of North American Birds.* 5th ed. American Ornithologists' Union.

Beardslee, Clark S., and Mitchell, Harold D. 1965. *Birds of the Niagara Frontier Region.* Buffalo: Bulletin of the Buffalo Society of Natural Science.

Beebe, Frank L. 1974. *Field Studies of the Falconiformes of British Columbia.* Victoria: The British Columbia Provincial Museum.

Beebe, Frank Lyman, and Webster, Harold Melvin. 1964. *North American Falconry & Hunting Hawks.* Denver: North American Falconry and Hunting Hawks.

Benson, S. Vere. 1965. *The Observer's Book of Birds.* London: Frederick Warne & Co. Ltd.

Bent, Arthur Cleveland. 1961. *Life Histories of North American Birds of Prey.* Vols. I & II. New York: Dover Publications, Inc.

Blanchan, Neltje. 1898. *Birds That Hunt and are Hunted.* New York: Grosset & Dunlap, Inc.

~ 1917. *Birds Worth Knowing.* Garden City: Doubleday, Page & Co.

Bond, James. 1971. *Birds of the West Indies.* London: William Collins Sons & Co. Ltd.

Brown, Leslie. 1970. *African Birds of Prey.* London: William Collins Sons & Co. Ltd.

~ 1976. *Birds of Prey.* London: The Hamlyn Publishing Group Ltd.

~ and Amadon, Dean. 1968. *Eagles, Hawks and Falcons of the World.* 2 vols. New York: McGraw-Hill Ryerson Ltd.

Bruun, Bertel. 1971. *Birds of Europe.* New York: Western Publishing Co., Inc.

Caley, Neville W. 1973. *What Bird Is That?* Sydney: Angus & Robertson Publishers.

Cameron, H. 1971. *The Nighwatchers.* New York: Four Winds Press.

Chapman, Frank M. 1932. *Handbook of Birds of Eastern North America.* New York: D. Appleton & Co.

Clements, James F. 1974. *Birds of the World: A Check List.* New York: The Two Continents Publishing Group, Ltd.

Collins, Henry Hill, Jr. 1959. *Complete Guide to American Wildlife.* New York: Harper & Row, Publishers, Inc.

Craighead, F., and Craighead, J. 1956. *Hawks, Owls and Wildlife.* Harrisburg: Stackpole Books.

Cruickshank, Allan D. 1954. *The Pocket Guide to the Birds.* New York: Pocket Books.

Eckert, Allan W. 1974. *The Owls of North America.* New York: Doubleday & Co., Inc.

Evans, Humphrey. 1960. *Falconry for You.* Newton Centre: Charles T. Branford Company.

Everett, Michael. 1977. *A Natural History of Owls.* London: The Hamlyn Publishing Group Ltd.

Falla, R. A.; Sibson, R. B.; and Turbott, E. G. 1970. *A Field Guide to the Birds of New Zealand.* London: William Collins Sons & Co. Ltd.

Felix, Jiri. 1975. *A Colour Guide to Familiar Garden and Field Birds' Eggs and Nests.* London: Octopus Books Ltd.

Fisher, James, and Peterson, Roger Tory. 1964. *World of Birds.* Garden City: Doubleday & Co., Inc.

Fitter, Richard, cons. ed. 1973. *Book of British Birds.* London: Driver Publications Ltd.

Forbush, Edward Howe. 1939. *Natural History of the Birds of Eastern and Central North America.* Boston: Houghton Mifflin Company.

Freeman, Richard. 1975. *Classification of the Animal Kingdom.* London: Lion Publishing.

Godrey, W. Earl. 1966. *The Birds of Canada.* Ottawa: National Museum of Canada.

Grossman, Mary Louise, and Hamlet, John. 1964. *Birds of Prey of the World.* New York: Clarkson N. Potter, Inc.

Grosvenor, Gilbert, and Wetmore, Alexander. eds. 1937. *The Book of Birds.* 2 vols. Washington: National Geographic Society.

Gruson, Edward S. 1972. *Words for Birds.* New York: Quadrangle Books.

~ 1976. *Checklist of the World's Birds.* New York: Quadrangle Books.

Guigust, C. J. 1973. *Birds of British Columbia (7) Owls.* Victoria: British Columbia Provincial Museum.

Hamerstrom, Frances. 1972. *Birds of Prey of Wisconsin.* Madison: The Wisconsin Society for Ornithology.

Harrison, Colin. 1978. *A Field Guide to the Nests, Eggs and Nestlings of North American Birds.* Glasgow: Wm Collins Publishers Pty Ltd.

Headstrom, Richard. 1970. *A Complete Field Guide to Nests in the United States.* New York: Ives Washburn, Inc.

Heintzelman, Donald S. 1979. *Hawks and Owls of North America.* New York: Universe Books.

Heinzel, Herman; Fitter, Richard; and Parslow, John. 1972. *The Birds of Britain and Europe.* London: William Collins Sons & Co. Ltd.

Henshaw, Henry W. 1918. *The Book of Birds.* Washington: National Geographic Society.

Hill, Robin. 1970. *Australian Birds.* Melbourne: Thomas Nelson, Inc.

Hogner, Dorothy Childs. 1969. *Birds of Prey.* New York: Thomas Y. Crowell Co.

Kieran, John. 1965. *An Introduction to Birds.* New York: Doubleday & Co., Inc.

Lansdowne, J.F. 1976. *Birds of the West Coast, I.* Toronto: M. F. Feheley Publishers.

Livingston, John H. 1966. *Birds of the Northern Forest.* Toronto: McClelland & Stewart Ltd.

~ 1968. *Birds of the Eastern Forest: I.* Toronto: McClelland & Stewart Ltd.

Mathews, F. Schuyler. 1921. *Field Book of Wild Birds and their Music.* New York: G. P. Putnam's Sons.

May, John Bichard. 1935. *The Hawks of North America.* New York: The National Association of Audubon Societies.

Michel, E. B. 1964. *The Art and Practice of Hawking.* Boston: Charles T. Brantford Co.

Pearson, T. Gilbert, ed. 1936. *Birds of America.* New York: Garden City Books.

Peterson, Roger Tory. 1939. *A Field Guide to the Birds.* Boston: Houghton Mifflin Company.

~ 1957. *How to Know the Birds.* New York: The New American Library.

~ 1961. *A Field Guide to Western Birds.* Boston: Houghton Mifflin Company.

~ 1963. *A Field Guide to the Birds of Texas and Adjacent States.* Boston: Houghton Mifflin Company.

~, et al. 1973. *The Birds.* New York: Time-Life Books.

~, and Chalif, Edward L. 1973. *A Field Guide to Mexican Birds.* Boston: Houghton Mifflin Company.

~, Mountfort, Guy and Hollom, P. A. D. *A Field Guide to the Birds of Britain and Europe.* Boston: Houghton Mifflin Company.

Pough, Richard H. 1949. *Audubon Land Bird Guide.* Garden City: Doubleday & Co., Inc.

~ 1951. *Audubon Water Bird Guide.* Garden City: Doubleday & Co., Inc.

~ 1957. *Audubon Western Bird Guide.* Garden City: Doubleday & Co., Inc.

Reed, Chester A. 1965. *North American Birds' Eggs.* New York: Dover Publications, Inc.

Reilly, Edgar M., Jr. 1968. *The Audubon Illustrated Handbook of American Birds.* New York: McGraw-Hill Ryerson, Inc.

Robbins, Chandler S.; Bruun, Bertel; and Zim, Herbert S. 1966. *Birds of North America.* New York: Golden Press.

Roberts, Thomas S. 1960. *Bird Portraits in Color*. Minneapolis: University of Minnesota Press.

Salt, W. Ray, and Salt, Jim R. 1976. *The Birds of Alberta*. Edmonton: Hurtig Publishers.

Samson, Jack. 1976. *Falconry Today*. New York: Henry Z. Walck, Inc.

Saunders, Areta A. 1935. *A Guide to Bird Songs*. New York: D. Appleton-Century Co. Inc.

Snyder, L. L. 1932. *The Hawks and Owls of Ontario*. Toronto: Royal Ontario Museum of Zoology.

~ 1951. *Ontario Birds*. Toronto: Clarke, Irwin & Co. Ltd.

~ 1957. *Arctic Birds of Canada*. Toronto: University of Toronto Press.

Sparks, John, and Spoer, Tony. 1970. *Owls Their Natural and Unnatural History*. New York: Taplinger Publishing Co.

Sprunt, Alexander, Jr. 1955. *North American Birds of Prey*. New York: Bonanza Books.

Taverner, P. A. 1934. *Birds of Canada*. Ottawa: National Museum of Canada.

Todd, W. E. Clyde. 1963. *Birds of the Labrador Peninsula and Adjacent Areas*. Toronto: Carnegie Museum and University of Toronto Press.

Tufts, Robie W. 1961. *The Birds of Nova Scotia*. Halifax: Nova Scotia Museum.

Van Tyne, Josselyn, and Berger, Andrew J. 1961. *Fundamentals of Ornithology*. New York: John Wiley & Sons, Inc.

Wallace, George J. 1955. *An Introduction to Ornithology*. New York: Macmillan, Inc.

Welty, Joel Carl. 1962. *The Life of Birds*. Philadelphia: W. B. Saunders Company.

Wetmore, Alexander, et al. 1965. *Water, Prey, and Game Birds of North America*. Washington: National Geographic Society.

Zim, Herbert S., and Gabrielson, Ira N. 1956. *Birds*. New York: Golden Press.

This book was designed by Frank Newfeld. It was typeset by Trigraph, Inc., Toronto, printed by Ashton-Potter Limited, Toronto, from film and colour separations supplied by herzig-sommerville ltd., Toronto. *North American Birds of Prey* was bound by the Hunter Rose Company Ltd., Toronto.

The typeface chosen is *Aldine Bembo*, first cut in 1495 by F. Griffi for Aldus Manutius.

The text is printed on *Beckett Text Laid*, and the plate sections on *Flokote Coated*.

The book is bound in *Bayside Linen*.